MID-LIFE CAREER RESCUE: JOB SEARCH STRATEGIES THAT WORK

HOW TO CONFIDENTLY LEAVE A JOB YOU HATE AND START LIVING A LIFE YOU LOVE, BEFORE IT'S TOO LATE

CASSANDRA GAISFORD

CONTENTS

EXCERPT: MID-LIFE CAREER RESCUE (EMPLOY YOURSELF)

COPYRIGHT

purchased for your use only, please respect the author's hard work and purchase your own copy.

Cover adapted from design by Ida Fia Sveningsson

Published by Blue Giraffe Publishing 2018

See our complete catalogue on Amazon at
Author.to/CassandraGaisford and www.cassandragaisford.com
ISBN eBook 978-0-9951081-6-5
ISBN Print 978-0-9951081-7-2
First Edition

Neither the publisher nor the author is engaged in rendering professional advice or services to the individual reader. The ideas, procedures, and suggestions contained in this book are not intended as a substitute for psychotherapy, counseling, or consulting with your physician.

Neither the author nor the publisher shall be liable or responsible for any loss or damage allegedly arising from any information or suggestion in this book.

FREE WORKBOOK!

Thank you for your interest in my new book.

To show my appreciation, I'm excited to be giving you another book for FREE!

Download the free *Find Your Passion Workbook* here: http://worklifesolutions.leadpages.co/free-find-your-passion-workbook.

I hope you enjoy it—it's dedicated to helping you live and work with passion, resilience and joy.

PRAISE FOR MID-LIFE CAREER RESCUE:EMPLOY YOURSELF

"More and more people today, either through choice or necessity, are looking for new and more fulfilling ways of working and earning their livings. Old ways are breaking down. Today, sacrificing your deeper passions for the security of a paycheck is no guarantee of security. Following your heart and deeper self is the new security. In this book, Cassandra helps you find your work, inspiring you to consider new possibilities, gently guiding you beyond limiting thinking, and helping you find your own true self and authentic work."

~ **Nick Williams, Author of** *The Work We Were Born to Do: Find the Work You Love, Love the Work You Do*

"I was curious about the content of this book, **Mid-Life Career Rescue: Job Search Strategies that Work,** as I have worked as a careers professional for almost 20 years and with a few variations on job search strategies over the years, my practise and coaching in this area of career coaching has remained largely the same. I wondered if the ideas, the suggestions, exercises and the theories that support these that I leaned all those years ago still held true. Did my ideas that I encourage my clients to undertake, still work, were they still in vogue even? Did my ideas need a complete over-haul? I looked to this book in the hope that it would help me face today's practises and update my own knowledge. So, with my curiosity in full openness I began to read.

First I was struck by the relevance of my knowledge to what Cassandra was suggesting in 2018. What I have been coaching my clients to do while exploring their own job search journey were still very useful. Second I was encouraged and even felt embraced by the strategies suggested in Cassandra's book for my own profes-sional re-development process that I am undertaking. Everything I am quietly doing to re-define my working and private life are here in black and white and gloriously celebrated as the way forward.

Cassandra has beautiful ideas, encouraging real life stories, and powerful and yet very accessible exercises to offer anyone who is either embarking on a job search journey or for anyone already on the journey but looking for further strategies to add new energy to their journey. **Mid-Life Career Rescue: Job Search Strategies that Work** is a book for job seekers and career professionals alike.

~ **Catherine Sloan, Counselor**

"Stop. Don't leave your job until you've read this book. Each chapter focuses on one highly practical aspect of changing careers."

~ **Barry Watson, Author of #1 bestseller *Relationship Rehab***

"This book has given me another kick up the bum, to write it all down, work from the end result backward, envisage the 'as if' and build the staircase I need to climb."

~ **Cate Walker, 5-Star Review**

"Makes you think and offers strategies to make it work! I met

Cassandra about 17 years ago after being made redundant—the advice she gave me and the challenges she threw at me even then have remained in my psyche and continue to give me motivation. So reading her books it's easy to hear her voice, continuing on with that motivation. I usually skip reading other people's stories as many of them don't translate to real life for me. But many in this book resonated, in particular, the opportunity that I have to follow not just one passion, but I can follow all three, and make them work! With ageism alive and well, I've had so many rejections for job opportunities that it's a matter of survival that you have to tread your own path—find opportunities for yourself. This book has given me the confidence that I CAN make it work."

   ~ **L.A. Brown, 5-Star Review**

"This book is written as though the author is in your living room, holding your hand, and giving you the courage to take the next small step. I have recommended it to more people than I can count."

   ~ **Sheree Clark, Health Living Coach, Fork In The Road**

*The tiny, brilliantly colorful hummingbird
symbolizes the messages in this book.*

*This versatile soul, despite its size,
is capable of unbelievable feats.
It can hover in mid-air, fly forwards, backwards,
side-ways, and even upside down.
Its rapidly beating wings can flap as high as 200 times per second,
enabling it to travel faster than a car.*

*The laws of physics say it should be impossible.
But the hummingbird does it anyway.*

I dedicate this book to those of you
who are ready to live a life more colorful,
and to do what others may say cannot be done.

This book is also for Lorenzo, my Templar Knight,
who encourages and supports me
to make my dreams possible…

And for all my clients
who've shared their dreams with me,
and allowed me to help them achieve amazing feats.

Thank you
for inspiring me.

FREEDOM

When a bird gets free,
it does not go back for remnants
left on the bottom of the cage.

Rumi

ABOUT THIS BOOK

When you're a mature worker and you find yourself in a position where you have to look for work, age bias can be a factor, but it doesn't have to be a barrier. Although some employers might look for young, less mature hires, older workers have lots to offer, as many smart organizations realize. Successfully finding a job takes skill, but once you know the rules, you'll feel more confident and a whole lot happier.

To increase your job search effectiveness this book will help you:

- Beat "age bias"
- Increase your awareness of the importance of self-marketing
- Highlight the appropriate attitudes, styles and behaviors that you will need to market your skills successfully
- Identify your natural knacks and talents which have commercial value.

- Prepare you to use a variety of job search strategies, including: Using recruitment agencies effectively; Responding to direct advertizing, including newspaper and Internet mediums; Outline the steps to successful networking; Provide strategies that will help maintain a positive outlook
- Build hope and confirm there is no better time for you to change your job or career
- Help you find and get the job or career you want

Some people find job hunting very challenging. Perhaps years of conditioning that you should be seen and not heard, acute shyness or lack of practice and experience in the art of self-promotion may be affecting you.

Have no fear, like any skill, this can be learned.

In *Mid-Life Career Rescue: Job Search Strategies That Work* you will also discover how to:

- Harness the law of attraction by focusing on areas of passion and purpose
- Tap into the hidden job market
- Let people know what you have to offer confidently
- Strengthen your creative thinking skills, and ability to identify possible roles you will enjoy
- Consider self-employment as a viable and fulfilling career

This book is divided into three sections. The first section will help you identify what's most important to you in a role. This is an important step. Too often people focus prematurely on sending out their resume, and applying for jobs without really knowing what makes them happy and what natural talents and employable skills they have to offer.

Employers are attracted to people who can do the job but importantly, job seekers who will be happy in their work. Very often employers will take on a candidate who may lack experience but who more than makes up for it with their passion and enthusiasm.

The first section will also help you reframe any concerns or unhelpful beliefs you may have about your age.

Let's look briefly at which each chapter in this book will cover.

Where there is a problem there is a cure. **Chapter One, "Unhappiness at Work,"** will help you identify the key causes of your job dissatisfaction. We will turn negatives into positives by adopting a solutions-focused approach to resolving current concerns.

This chapter will help you gain greater clarity about what you want to change and how to direct your energies positively toward your preferred future.

You'll gain greater insight into your personal passions, and criteria for job satisfaction. Knowing these things will help you begin the process of creating and attracting your dream role.

Research suggests that many mid-lifers have a negative expectancy about their ability to find meaningful work. **Chapter Two, "The Gift of Longevity,"** will highlight the opportunities that demographic and social shifts have created for mature employees.

Activities in this chapter, and emphasising age as an asset, will help strengthen your self-belief and confidence, and overcome any lingering doubts about re-inventing your life at your age and life stage. This will enable you to target your job hunting activities positively.

Traditional career paths are fast disappearing and the jobs of the future have yet to be invented. **Chapter Three, "It All Begins with**

an Idea," highlights the role of creativity in defining and finding the work you want to do.

This chapter will introduce you to some creative, yet practical, techniques that will help you gain greater clarity about what inspires and excites you and begin the process of finding your best-fit career.

Many people think that unless they have a formal qualification, or recent work experience, they don't have any skills. **Chapter Four, "Valuing Natural Knacks and Talents,"** will boost awareness of your natural gifts and innate abilities and strengths.

As one of my clients who hated her job told me, "I'm good at what I do, and people keep promoting me, but does anybody ask me if enjoy it?" Importantly, this chapter will also help you to identify your favorite skills, the activities that bring you joy and how to focus your job search activities in light of your enthusiasms.

Section Two will introduce you to practical job hunting strategies, including using networks, social media, and traditional methods of job hunting, including using recruitment firms and responding to job ads effectively. You'll also gain practical skills in informational interviewing which will help you tap into the hidden job market effectively.

Chapter Five, "Developing a Self-Marketing Plan", will summarize common job search techniques and highlight those that are most effective. You'll also discover some effective steps to help you prepare a successful job search marketing plan.

By far the most successful job search technique is the process of networking—using personal contacts to uncover the "hidden" job market. **Chapter Six, "Networking: Discovering the Hidden Job Market"**, will arm you with powerful, simple and effective ways to use this strategy confidently.

Many job seeker misunderstand the role of recruitment agencies and consultants. As a former recruitment agent for a large global consultancy in **Chapter Seven, "Recruitment Agents/Consultants",** I share a a few "facts" to help you.

Chapter Eight, "Responding to Advertisements", will help you master the practical aspects of responding to advertised positions, including how to write cover letters and ensure your CV or resume effectively communicates your fit and ensures you make it to the interview stage.

Chapter Nine, "Internet Job Search Strategies" , will help you use social media and online job portals effectively, including how to avoid being banished to the "slush pile."

Help you keep track of your job search activities is the focus of **Chapter Ten.**

Job hunting can be stressful and full of setbacks. Staying optimistic, exercising excellent self-care, and maintaining a positive mindset is a critical skill and the focus of the **Section Three.** You'll also be encouraged to consider and explore self-employment, consulting, or starting your own business as the ultimate career.

Chapter 11, "Stress Less," will help you develop effective strategies to manage any current stress you may be experiencing. Very often getting rid of stressors, and restoring some balance, can led you to fall back in love with a job you've begun to hate.

It will also provide you with some useful tools to help you build resilience throughout the change and job hunting.

Developing the psychological "muscle" that will get you through the rough spots as you embark on your job search is the focus of **Chapter 12: Staying Positive.**

Finally**, in Chapter 13, "Be Your Own Boss",** (lucky 13), I share an excerpt from the third book in the *Mid-Life Career Rescue* series, Employ Yourself. Sometimes, despite all your skills, all your best efforts, and all your optimistic "hire me" manifesting, you struggle to land a job.

This can be a blessing in disguise as many "unemployable" people testify. It took a good dose of adversity to get Wendy Pye's entrepreneurial juices flowing and she hasn't looked back. She was dumped without warning from NZ News after 22 years with the company, given five minutes to clear her desk, and then marched off the premises.

With no job to go to Pye, then aged 42, set up her own educational publishing company. Now a multi-millionaire, she admits her motivation for going it alone was a desire to show her former employers what she could do.

"I was devastated and disappointed. But it really changed my life, which is a lot better now than if [redundancy] had never happened. I needed the push."

She certainly showed her former employers just what she could do. The 2015 National Business Review's Rich List, estimates Pye's personal wealth at $105 million.

How To Use This Book

Mid-Life Career Rescue: Job Search Strategies That Work takes the stress out of changing careers by tapping into the power of creativity and out of the box thinking. Right from the start it will stretch your awareness of what you think is possible.

This book will help you make informed career choices that allow you to be true to yourself and that stand the test of time.

It provides a systematic, structured and inspirational way to facilitate both self- and career-awareness, and to help you have faith in yourself and confidence in your decisions.

The key components of determining what you want to do and what others will pay you to do are presented in bite-sized portions that make it much easier to assimilate.

Journal exercises, inspiring quotations and many other simple but effective tools to feed your inspiration and boost your confidence will help feed your desire for a new, improved life.

Throughout this book you'll be encouraged to make positive changes in your life, step by step, by applying the strategies discussed. You may want to create a special journal, notebook or use a digital tool to make a few notes and apply the tools and techniques I've designed especially for you.

My aim is to make *Mid-Life Career Rescue: Job Search Strategies That Work* as interactive as possible by combining a minimum of theory with a maximum of practical tools and techniques that you can apply to your own situation.

Your Virtual Coach

To really benefit from this book think of it as your 'virtual' coach – try the calls to action and additional exercises that you'll find in all the chapters.

These action tasks are designed to facilitate greater insight and to help you integrate new learnings. Resist the urge to just process them in your head. We learn best by doing. Research has proven time and time again that the act of writing deepens your knowledge and learning.

Writing down your insights is the area where people like motivational guru Tony Robbins say that the winners part from the losers, because the losers always find a reason not to write things down. Harsh but perhaps true!

You will also come across plenty of action questions. Open-ended questions are great thought provokers. Your answers to these questions will help you gently challenge current assumptions and gain greater clarity about your goals and desires.

If you are currently unemployed, or not in the paid workforce, you may find it helpful to think about your previous roles when completing the exercises.

Keeping A Passion Journal

A passion journal is also a great place to store sources of inspiration to support you through the career planning and change process. For some tips to help you create your own inspirational passion journal, go to the media page on my website and watch my television interview here >>

Passion Journal Tip Sheet

Every year I create a passion journal to help clarify and manifest my intentions. It's a fun and incredibly powerful process. I've created my dream job, a soul mate, our wonderful life style property, a publishing contract and more. Try it for yourself! Download my free tip sheet to help you create your own passion journal here >>

Inspirational Quotes

Sometimes all it takes is the slightest encouragement – one simple inspirational sentence – to launch oneself into a new and more satisfying orbit. I have included plenty of inspiration throughout the book and in the Career Rescue Community detailed below to help you do just that!

Surf The Net

Throughout the book I have included a selection of my e-Resources. These have been carefully selected to encourage further insight and to enable you to tap into regularly updated resources, including those created by me just for you.

There is no 'right' or 'wrong' way to work with *Mid-Life Career*

Rescue: Job Search Strategies That Work. It's a very flexible tool – the only requirement is that you use it in a way that meets your needs. For example, you may wish to work through the book and exercises sequentially. Alternatively, you may wish to work intuitively and complete the exercises in an ad hoc fashion. Or just start where you need to start.

Whilst it is recommended that the chapters and the exercises are worked through ign the order they appear, each chapter can be read independently. You may wish to read a chapter each week, fortnight or month. Or you may wish to use your intuition and select a page at random.

Web links throughout the book and the supplementary resources will help encourage further moments of insight, inspiration and clarity about the career path that's right for you.

Getting Started

Increasing your self-awareness is a crucial first step in moving toward the career of your dreams. Take the time to complete the following Job Search Quiz to evaluate where you are now.

JOB SEARCH QUIZZ

How effective is your current job search strategy?

Highlight your responses to the questions below:

The ways you have found a job in the past are by:

1. Responding to an advertisement in the newspaper
2. Responding to an advertisement on the Internet
3. Registering your resume on the Internet
4. Asking friends and colleagues
5. Cold calling an organization that you wanted to work for
6. All of the above

If you were hiring someone which strategy would you use to fill a job vacancy?

1. Place an advertisement in the newspaper
2. Place an advertisement on the Internet

3. Enlist the services of a recruitment agency
4. Use your professional and personal networks

Why would you use your preferred job strategy identified above?

1. Cost effective
2. Saves time
3. Minimize the risk of hiring the wrong person
4. You trust personal recommendations

Contacting people to find out if they know of any roles which might suit you, feels:

1. Terrifying —I would only do that as a last resort
2. Like begging—only people who are desperate do that
3. OK—it is a necessary and effective job search strategy

INTRODUCTION

"Research has proven that only 20% of all the positions available at any time are going to be advertised by Recruitment Consultants or directly by companies looking to employ someone."
~ Richard Bolles, author

Are you LOOKING for a job or waiting for one to come to you? Research has proven that only 20% of all the positions available at any time are going to be advertised by Recruitment Consultants or directly by companies looking to employ someone.

Unfortunately many people looking for their next role use what Richard Bolles, author of *What Colour Is Your Parachute*, refers to as the "Neanderthal Job Search Strategy".

The diagram below is an adaptation of this strategy—clearly illustrating that most job seekers put their energies into the least effective job hunt methods.

The Hidden Job Market

By far the most successful job-search technique is the process of networking—using personal contacts to uncover the "hidden" job market.

The hidden job market refers to those positions that are never advertised. Largely this technique is so successful because organizations also use their networks to find employees when vacancies occur—advertising is often a last resort.

The hidden job market can also refer to jobs that are created just for you. This was my experience following a period of what I call Informational Interviewing, which essentially involves researching careers and workplaces you maybe interested in and talking to staff or potential employers.

As I share in the first book in the *Mid-Life Career Rescue* series, *The Call For Change,* after talking with an organization whose values and purpose I admired and respected, they created a job tailor-made to my skillset and dreams. I share this powerful and simple strategy with you later in this book.

But first, let's explore how to clarify what you really want and need from a job to feel happy and fulfilled. If you're already clear on your non-negotiable criteria for job satisfaction feel free to skip ahead to Part Two: Getting The Job You Want.

PART I

WHAT JOB DO YOU WANT?

1

UNHAPPINESS AT WORK

SOMETIMES IN LIFE, as in photography, you need a negative to make a positive image of the life you want to capture.

Are you showing signs of job dissatisfaction? Did you wake up this morning excited to face the day ahead? Or did the thought of getting up and going to work make you wish you could stay in bed?

If Monday mornings are a low point in your week, it may be a sign that it's time for a new career.

Often you know what you want subconsciously before you know it consciously. While you may still be debating whether or not to stay in your job, your subconscious mind may have already decided it's time for you to move on.

You may be like so many of my clients who say, "I could do anything if only I knew what it was."

The exercises in this chapter and those following will help take the stress out of making a change, confirm your best-fit career and give you the confidence to move toward your preferred future.

A good place to start is to use current things getting you down as signposts to your preferred future. Sometimes in life, as in photography, you need a negative to make a positive.

Confirming what's causing your job blues will help you get clear about your intentions, options and possibilities.

Perhaps you're like many of my clients and wonder whether you, not your job, are the major cause of your unhappiness. Is it your attitude? Or is it your work that's making you feel trapped? Getting clear about who you are and what you need to feel happy and fulfilled is an important step in confirming exactly which one needs to change.

Carlos Castaneda, in his book *The Fire From Within*, teaches Don Juan about the need to take care before embarking on change, when he says, "To have a path of knowledge, a path with heart makes for a joyful journey and is the only conceivable way to live. We must then think carefully about our paths before we set out on them for by the time a person discovers that his path 'has no heart,' the path is ready to kill him. At that point few of us have the courage to abandon the path, lethal as it may be, because we have invested so much in it, and to choose a new path seems so danger-ous, even irresponsible. And so we continue dutifully, if joylessly along."

Tune Into Your Body Barometer

Liking what you do is not only a vital ingredient of career success but also health and mental well-being. When you don't do the things you love your health can suffer.

Common signs of neglecting your happiness and feeling trapped in a job that you don't enjoy can include:

- Headaches
- Insomnia
- Tiredness
- Depression
- Low self-esteem
- Lack of confidence
- Irritability and other warning signs.

YOU'LL BE able to identify your own warning signs in the chapter *Stress Less*, and identify some strategies to boost your resilience.

The main thing I want to emphasize now is that your body never lies; however, many people soldier on ignoring the obvious warning signs their body is giving them—until it's too late.

It's easy to rationalize these feelings away, but the reality is your body is screaming out for something different, something way better! Having the courage to say, "Enough" and to pursue a more satisfying alternative can seem daunting but the rewards and benefits that flow makes the effort so worthwhile.

PART OF BEING **a winner is knowing when to quit.**

Action Questions

Why do you need a job that makes you happy? What benefits will flow when you are living your passion? What happens when you ignore your passion?

Some Alarming Facts

* Less than 10% of people are visibly living their passion. Lack of passion, and career dissatisfaction, are common causes of stress, low productivity, poor performance and plummeting levels of confidence and self-esteem.

   * Lack of feedback, autocratic bosses, poor work-life balance, lack of control, values conflicts, low challenge, boredom, high workloads and interpersonal conflicts push happiness levels down on a daily basis for a large number of employees.

   * We all know that smoking kills but few people know that job strain is as bad as smoking according to researchers from the Harvard School of Public Health in Boston. They concluded that too often people rely on medication to tackle the job blues but one of the most effective cures would be to tackle the job environment.

   * Unhappiness at work is a major drain on individuals, organizations and the economy. One Canadian study argued that a 1% improvement through helping people become fully engaged in programs that lead them to find work they would love, would release an additional $600 million each year into the economy.

   * Many people have been conditioned to expect less from the world of work, and may have narrow expectations about the wealth of opportunity that now exists.

   * Unhappy people: complain more, produce less, get sick more often, worry more, have fewer creative ideas, have lower energy levels, are more pessimistic, less motivated, learn slower, make

poorer decisions, have lower confidence and self-esteem, are more prone to mental illnesses, including depression, and are slower to bounce back from setbacks—and these are only some of the symptoms of unhappiness.

No wonder unhappy people are exhausted.

Is It Time For A Change?

Change isn't always easy. It takes a lot of planning, effort and preparation. But the results are worth it. A well-planned change brings new beginnings, fresh experiences and a job that fulfills and energizes your life.

Despite all the positive benefits that a fresh start can bring, you may well find that until the pain of remaining the same hurts more than the effort required to change, it can be hard to get motivated.

Using your knowledge and clarity about what's causing your job blues will help you identify possible solutions, and tap into the powerful energy of intention to create positive changes.

The Positivity of Negativity

Setbacks can sometimes be opportunities in disguise. As you look back, times that seemed like low points can, with hindsight, prove to be the most life-changing and meaningful experiences. If your job is draining you this can prove challenging. It is hard to feel optimistic when you are depleted.

However, Viktor Frankl, an Austrian psychiatrist who survived the horrors of the Nazi death camps, believes that it's not the situation which defines and controls us, but our attitudes and reactions.

Somehow, he urges, we must endeavor to look for meaning and

purpose in situations that cause us to suffer. If after everything Viktor Frankl went though he can find something positive in the most horrific of situations, it's something you can do too.

The challenge, if you're up for it, is to constantly strive to look for the silver linings in stormy weather. For example, the fact that you are unhappy at work is a silver lining in disguise—it's the motivating force you need to make a change!

These same principles apply whether you're a stay-at-home-mom contemplating a return to work, or if you have been out of work for some time. By recalling the times you've been unhappy you'll gain greater clarity about what you need to feel happy at work. And vice versa.

Jasmine, a clinical psychologist once told me, "The job's just not me. I need a new one but I don't know what I want." By listing the things she didn't like, as well as the things she enjoyed in both her current and previous roles, she was better able to identify the things which were important to her. Building this list of criteria for job satisfaction helped her narrow where to begin her search.

Cultivating a Liberating Attitude

Thinking optimistically and living in constant gratitude for what you do have versus over-focusing on what you don't have increases confidence, hope, feelings of satisfaction and happiness—all necessary preparatory ingredients for positive transitions.

It is no coincidence that the successful people in life see the cup half full and look for ways to add more to people's lives, rather than demand or expect others top them up.

Successful, liberated people are also smart—they know how to accept the things they can't change and take control of the things they can.

Like any skill, cultivating a liberated attitude is something anyone can learn.

"THERE WILL COME a time when you believe everything is finished that will be the beginning" ~ Louis L'Amour, Author

Client Success Story: From Despair to Gratitude

Diana, hated her job so much the strain was beginning to take a toll. When she started her job as a designer for a large international company she thought it was great.

But the workload was excruciating—she soon found that she was doing a job that previously needed three people. She quickly felt overloaded and drained of energy.

The pressure was getting to her and she talked of being the sickest she had ever been in her life. She shared her feelings of frustration and admitted that she spent most of her day complaining about the things she didn't like about her job with her colleagues.

When she wasn't at work she moaned to her friends and to her partner. She wished she could say, 'I quit,' but couldn't afford to financially. Diana felt trapped.

Diana began to wonder if her illness was a direct result of feeling at 'dis-ease' with her job and sought career counseling to help her work out a cure.

I asked her how—given that she was not able to resign in the short term—she felt she could make her current work situation more bearable, even enjoyable.

She found generating ideas hard and couldn't think of any possible solutions. I encouraged her to buy a journal and write down all the things about her current job she was grateful for. This threw her a bit!

After a particularly bad day she drew up her list which included:

that she was employed and had a steady wage; earned overtime for extra hours; worked close to where she lived; had access to great products and services; had six weeks paid leave; and that she liaised with international buyers and people at the top of their field that she could learn from.

After completing this list Diana said she felt immediately *"lighter"* and better about her job. She began to see what a vicious self-fulfilling cycle her negative attitude to work was having and made a conscious decision to stop talking about what she didn't like.

She vowed to only speak in positive terms or not at all. As she began to feel happier and more energized Diana found it easier to see potential solutions to her career rut.

She put forward a proposal to redefine her job and responsibilities. This wasn't accepted by her boss, but rather than become negative and resentful Diana looked for the silver lining.

She felt that by not getting what she wanted she was being prompted to get clear about what she did want long term and to start preparing for the time when she would leave.

She set some goals and developed an action plan to bring more passion into both her private and personal life. Knowing that she was beginning to take some positive steps to move the detrimental out of her life and make room for the positive, and choosing to see obstacles as learning experiences, made her remaining time less painful.

One year later she set up her own design company. If the idea of being your own boss makes your soul sing, you'll find some helpful tips for self-employed success in my bestseller, Mid-Life Career Rescue (Employ Yourself).

What can you take away from this story? You don't always need to quit your job. Sometimes, you can resign your current role to find greater fulfilment.

"I truly believe that absent the victim mentality, everyone—regardless of background, education, or ability—can carve out a good path for themselves in this tumultuous workplace."
~ Richard Bolles, Author

Call to Action! Your Gratitudes

What's right about your career and life right now? Jot down some things that come to mind. Create a gratitude section in your passion journal and add to it regularly.

Client Success Story: From Problems To Solutions

Jeremy was feeling very frustrated in his job and talked constantly about all the things that weren't going well. Focusing on problems made him feel increasingly angry and frustrated.

His irritability and despondency began to take a negative toll on his self-esteem and confidence and infected his relationships with his boss and co-workers.

It was hard to contain his feelings to work, and before long his frustrations began to take a toll on his marriage. To shift him from a problems focus to a solutions focus, he wrote down the things that frustrated him and looked for the silver linings and opportunities for personal development that these things created.

Summaries of these are below. He created a list of 'action items' to help him prepare for and leverage off any opportunities, including making a time to speak to HR and his manager with the aim of creating development opportunities within his workplace. His preparation, including becoming more comfortable asking for his needs to be met, paid off and he was offered a secondment into a new division.

FRUSTRATION: My skills are unappreciated

Opportunity: I am learning that I need to be more comfortable 'blowing my own trumpet' and telling people what I have achieved

FRUSTRATION: All they do is talk about things—nothing gets done

Opportunity: I have the opportunity to listen, utilize and learn from people who have skills I want to develop

FRUSTRATION: Recognition is just related to money billed

Opportunity: I need to take responsibility for communicating my own career drivers and suggesting some other ways that I would like to be rewarded for my efforts

FRUSTRATION: My boss is a bully

Opportunity: I am learning how to stand up for myself and not be intimidated by 'challenging' personalities. Knowledge is power and I seek help from people who know how to deal with these issues

FRUSTRATION: I'm bored

Opportunity: The lack of challenge is motivating me to feel the fear and do it anyway—i.e., leave and find a new job that stretches me

Call to Action! Your Silver Linings

Create your own record of possible silver linings and notice how your energy shifts and how you begin to feel as you move from focusing on problems to looking for solutions. Continue the exercise in your passion journal whenever you feel frustrated or discouraged.

The Courage to Define What You Want

It may feel easier to go for the comfortable option when thinking about a career change. You may feel you lack energy, or confidence, to set your sights higher. Or you may feel you face very real barriers to employment, and lack the drive and self-belief to overcome setbacks.

In all my years of career counseling the biggest barrier I've found when working with clients is helping them believe they can manifest their dreams.

Fear of disappointment and even of success often underlies many peoples' reluctance to define what they want. As one of my clients said, "If I tell you my dream I might realize I can't achieve it. Then not only will I have failed but I'll have lost my dream."

Failure to set and follow through on career goals is one of the biggest reasons that only 10% of people are visibly pursuing their passion, and why well over 63% of people are dissatisfied with their work.

Using insights gained from this chapter and the exercises in the following chapters will help you have the courage to define what you want and develop the mindset and skills to achieve it.

AFFIRM WHAT YOU WANT!

ONCE YOU ARE clear about the forces that drive your decisions, finding a job that you like is easier. It won't happen overnight but it will happen! But first you need to get clear about what your perfect job would look like.

Call to Action! Your Criteria For Job Satisfaction

In your passion journal or notebook head up a page: "Criteria for Job Satisfaction." Re-frame any of the negative statements you identified in the dissatisfaction quiz at the beginning of this chapter into positive statements about what you *do* want.

You may also want to include a brief statement about why it is important to you. For example, if you wrote: "I get no feedback," write something like, "I want to receive feedback on a regular basis. This is important to me because I want to feel valued and to know that what I have done is appreciated."

Add to this list all the things about your current job or previous jobs that you've enjoyed. Don't worry if you don't have many things on your list. This is only the beginning and as you work through some of the exercises in the rest of the series you will gain more ideas about all the ingredients that make a job satisfying to you.

From Strain To Gain

When I first decided on a career as a recruitment consultant I thought it would be a great opportunity to help people find jobs they enjoyed and to use my coaching skills.

I didn't realize that the major part of the job was sales and business development. The seeds of dissatisfaction festered as I realized that I was not using the skills that I enjoyed.

In addition, the things that were really important to me, such as the value I placed on helping people, were compromised. It was a sales culture where the commission earned by putting people into

jobs or a workplace, that I knew wasn't a good fit, was more important than helping people find the *right* job.

For a long time I tried to ignore my unhappiness. Finding
another job seemed like too much work and secretly I couldn't help
but wonder if maybe I expected too much from my job. Shouldn't I
be grateful to have an income? My self-esteem plummeted and I felt
too frightened to look for another job—what if nobody else
wanted me?

Before long my growing 'dis-ease' with my job bubbled out into
painful blisters. I was quickly diagnosed with shingles.

Until I'd experienced what it was like not to do what I enjoyed I
didn't realize how important these things were to me. I started to
look for ways to do more of what I wanted and less of what I didn't.
When the opportunity came to move into the career management
team I leapt at the chance. I enjoyed it but I still didn't get to do
what I really wanted—hands on coaching.

Several years later, with my eye to the future, I left the company
altogether and aligned myself with a role much more in tune with
my soul and my longer-term goals.

Then later still I left the security of that salaried job and
embraced the freedom of self-employment and owning my own
business. I was a single mum—the sole breadwinner—with a mortgage. There was no safety net other than the preparation I'd done
and the belief and knowledge that I had salable skills which were in
demand. I've never looked back.

Saying Hello And Goodbye

Some of the things I said hello to when I made a move were
increased freedom, autonomy and earnings. I said goodbye to being
controlled, and having a cap on my salary.

While there were trade-offs, such as no longer having paid

annual leave and statutory holidays, the benefits, including the
ability to work from home and the flexibility to care for my
daughter—especially during her school holidays—more than
compensated for any losses.

ACTION TASK! Hello-Goodbye

Say hello to your preferred future and goodbye to the past by
creating your own hello-goodbye list in your passion journal.
Remember to include the benefits you'll gain by releasing what no
longer serves you. Add to this list as you gain more insights from
the exercises in the following chapter:

SURF THE NET

Listen to my interview on Radio New Zealand, and hear more
about being happy at work.Click here >>

*"CHANGE IS the end result of all true learning. Change involves
three things: First, a dissatisfaction with self—a felt void or need;
second, a decision to change—to fill the void or need; and third, a
conscious dedication to the process of growth and change—the
willful act of making the change; Doing Something."* ~ Dr Phil

DISSATISFACTION QUIZ

BEFORE YOU FIND the cure to your job blues you first need to get
clear about what's causing the problem. The following Dissatisfaction Quiz will help.

Perhaps you can identify with some of the common causes of dissatisfaction below. In your journal record (or highlight in your eBook) the statements below that are true for you. You may find that this is a useful starting point in identifying what needs to change in order to be happy at work. Your answers can also highlight which parts or books in the series will be most helpful to you.

1. You don't know what your skills are or what you're good at
2. Lack of recognition—people don't value you and what you do
3. You're bored and your job lacks challenge—you can't see any opportunity for growth or advancement
4. The culture is very negative
5. You don't get on with your co-workers
6. You feel stuck and can't see a way to make any improvements
7. You keep getting looked over for promotion
8. You don't know what makes you happy
9. You're not doing the things that really matter to you
10. The job doesn't meet your values
11. Your life feels out of balance
12. The workload is too heavy
13. Your job pays the bills but your passions are left as a hobby
14. You have a growing sense—vague though it might be— that you could improve the quality of your life
15. You have very little autonomy and control over your work
16. Your role or organization isn't spiritually aligned to the things you believe in
17. Office politics get you down

18. Your job and/or work environment is not fun
19. People don't have pride in their work, and poor performance is often ignored
20. Your wages are too low
21. The organization is too bureaucratic—policies and procedures slow everything down
22. You're not using the skills you enjoy
23. You feel 'boxed' in and don't know how to get into something different
24. You don't know what you want to do
25. Only the bosses' ideas are listened to
26. Your job lacks security
27. Very little about the job interests you
28. You have lost your confidence and your self-esteem is low
29. You're not achieving your potential
30. You park the 'real you' at the door—the robotic you goes to work
31. Personal issues are impacting on your enjoyment of work—these issues affect your focus, and motivation, etc.
32. The work environment isn't very attractive
33. Lack of training and support makes it difficult to do your job well
34. People are bullied and/or not treated with respect
35. Your role lacks meaning and purpose—you don't feel that what you contribute makes a difference

SCORING:

0-6 Congratulations! Nothing really seems to be getting you

down. Perhaps you're just looking for a new challenge. Read on for tips and strategies to help you move in a new direction.

6-20 if you answered "yes" to 6 or more of these statements you are moderately dissatisfied with the way things are going in your life. Develop specific actions for identifying and incorporating passion into your life.

21-35 You are suffering from severe dissatisfaction. You really do deserve to pursue a more satisfying alternative. Take immediate steps now to create positive changes in your work and life. In addition to applying the strategies in this book you may wish to solicit the support of a professional.

What You've Learned So Far

- The job-blues can be a powerful motivating force for change. By putting the spotlight on what you don't want, the sources of your unhappiness can point you in the direction of your heart's desire.
- Looking for the silver linings can help you transform a crisis into an opportunity.
- The body barometer never lies. Feelings of tiredness and activities that drain you are signs that you are settling for less. Feelings of depression, boredom and lifelessness are signs from your intuition that you are ignoring your passion. Take time to reprioritize your life and focus on what gives you energy and happiness, and start letting go of everything that drains you.
- Happiness isn't something that just happens—it's something we actively participate in creating. There's no better place to start than training your mind, and shaping your attitude—even when life turns to lumpy

custard you'll still manage to find something to be grateful for.

- Take control—feeling helpless, accepting the unacceptable, and procrastinating about taking action can lead to feelings of depression, hopelessness and quickly erode your confidence. Taking action will quickly help to get rid of the job blues.
- Your mind has the power to influence your reality. As you begin to envision your preferred future, notice how your dreams and intentions begin to not only influence your attitudes and actions, but how it will reach and influence the circumstances of your life. All things are created twice—first mentally and then physically.
- The desire for a better life and maintaining a positive expectancy will give you the motivational kickstart you need to break out of your rut and pursue the happiness you deserve.

WHAT'S NEXT?

In the next chapter we're going to look at why it's a great time to be a mid-lifer and look at ways to reframe any mistaken beliefs you, or those you want to work for, may have about being at your age and stage.

"TO THE POOR old mid-life worker, it can seem like nothing is possible. The reality is nothing could be further from the truth. People are changing jobs and starting new lives continually." ~ Fitzsimons and Beckford, Authors

2

THE GIFT OF LONGEVITY

IT IS a great time for mid-lifers to make the leap to a new career, but for some people, this means reframing their expectations of employment.

Embracing the new world of work, where it seems likely that many people will continue to work in paid employment into their late 60s, 70s and beyond means a mindset change for not just employers but also, more importantly, for individuals themselves.

Many countries and organizations are facing a critical skills shortage as fewer and fewer younger people enter the workforce and mature workers continue to opt out of mainstream employment.

Among these messages of impending disaster at a conference I attended in Italy it was refreshing to hear delegates from France, Italy and Australia reframe the issues from a problem to an opportunity and to speak about positive aging and the "gift of longevity."

But so many of the more 'mature' clients I coach still feel their age is a problem. They worry that they are too old to change careers, and despair they have left it too late to change.

"My life has been a life of regret," one of my clients said. At the ripe young age of 45, he couldn't see much hope of improving his situation.

Similarly, Mike, a professional man in his late 50s told me he was too old to change career. He also worried that employers would feel the same way. After reading this book and some follow up coaching he changed his mindset and opportunities flooded his way.

He's now working in a role that his friends say looks like it was tailor-made just for him.

"Some really great news—I've just heard I got the job I went after. Can hardly believe it after trying to find a way into this area of work for a long time. For me it's confirmation of the importance and power of managing my thought processes," he wrote.

Worryingly it's not just older workers that have pessimistic job expectations. "Don't you do what you love when you retire?" one 25-year-old client asked me. I was stunned. "Where did you learn that?" I asked. "It's what my mother told me," she confessed.

"MID-LIFE IS a time to reinvent ourselves and make new choices based on what we truly want. The challenge is to look at the changing energy with anticipation. We can throw away the roles

that do not serve and open to ones that contain more freedom to be ourselves. " ~Barbara Biziou, Author

Are You Stuck In The Dark Ages?

Authors of *You Don't Make a Big Leap Without a Gulp: Having the Courage to Change Careers and Live Again*, Mike Fitzsimons and Nigel Beckford, suggest that many people are trapped in a Depression-era mindset, thinking, "I'm lucky to have a job," or "I'll sit it out until I retire."

An article in *Time Magazine* also confirmed the reality that many mature workers have been conditioned to expect less from the world of work. As a result, they often have negative views or expectations about the wealth of opportunity that now exists.

The reality is that there's a huge amount of opportunity out there for people wanting more from their working lives than to grit their teeth and bear it, and for those who want to gain greater financial security. As Eleanor Roosevelt once said, "The future belongs to those who believe in the beauty of their dreams."

Breaking Free

The greatest challenge we mid-lifers have is to actively break free from narrow views of what is possible and embrace a sense of adventure.

To gain the courage to change careers and the skills to hunt for jobs successfully requires the ability and willingness to challenge assumptions.

Changing careers mid-life also requires a healthy dose of inspiration, a commitment to careful planning and the willingness to take calculated risks.

Now is the perfect time to rekindle a sense of adventure and embrace the wealth of opportunity that exists for mature people in the workforce.

However research suggests that people spend more time looking after their teeth and monitoring their cholesterol levels, and servicing their cars but neglect to spend time having regular career checks.

Does this sound like you? If so, where and how do you start planning your mid-life career transition?

Embracing The New World of Possibilities

The Association of Career Professionals International says that adopting a creative and lateral approach to career and work choices is the key to embracing the new world of possibilities.

They urge vocational guidance practitioners to encourage clients to be imaginative when thinking about ways to combine skills, talents, and interests to secure paid employment.

But being creative isn't the way many mid-lifers have been encouraged to think about careers! You may have experienced the old narrow model of career decision-making where you were told what you could do. For example, women were told their choices were severely limited to roles such as nursing, teaching, typing or being a wife.

Or perhaps you've been conditioned to think a job has to be just one thing, and that this one thing, is something you only do from an office, from 9-5 or longer.

Thankfully for people today there are almost unlimited career choices, and various ways to bundle the work week.

Helping people like you think laterally and creatively about careers is my strength and my passion, but first, let's get you started thinking positively about your life stage.

The Changing World Of Work

Over the last 10 years, we have seen unprecedented change. Globalization and technological revolutions such as the Internet and mobile devices have made it so much easier for companies and individuals to generate income anywhere, anytime.

This has led to many benefits, including a wider variety of goods and services, and a diversity of employment scenarios. Now you have an increased ability to generate income from the comfort of your own home, and greater opportunities to live and work overseas.

Len, aged 54, runs a thriving recruitment business from the beautiful serenity of his lifestyle property. Sally lives on a neighboring property, using Skype, email, and her phone, is able to manage her very successful mortgage company.

And you don't have to be self-employed to benefit from technological and global advancements. Numerous businesses offer flexible working arrangements to attract and retain staff.

The increased level of commercial and competitive pressures has also meant that companies, and their employees, need to constantly re-invent themselves to keep up. This is great news for mid-lifers wanting to make a positive change.

The Changing World of Work Table

The list below highlights how some of these changes have impacted on work and careers. Add to this list any changes that you or those close to you have personally experienced or know of.

THE PAST	NOW
A job for life	Multiple jobs
Predictable career path	Varied career paths
Apprenticeships	Learn off the job/pay your own training
Loyalty to one organization	Loyalty to self
Narrowly defined role	Multitasking/project-based work
Managers	Leaders
Work with hands	Work with head/knowledge workers
Protected economy	Global economy/competition
Limited choices/opportunities	Unlimited choices/opportunities
Gender-specific roles	Gender-neutral roles
World stability/peace	World instability/conflict
Limited technology	Constantly changing technology
IQ	Emotional Intelligence (EQ)
Organisational hierarchies	Flat structures
Full employment	3rd generation unemployed
Stable organizations	Unstable organizations/restructuring
Full-time employment	Contract, part-time and portfolio work
Employee	Contractor
Stable workforce	High turnover of employees
Labor surplus	Labor shortage (changing demographics)
One-job (9-5)	Portfolio work/job combo
Job matching	Job creation/job sculpting
Tied to a location	Independent of location
Office/Bricks and Mortar	Virtual Office/Lifestyle Entrepreneur

CAN you think of any other changes impacting how we live and work? What new opportunities might any shifts in the world of work create for you?

Call to Action! Aging Positively

If you're like Mike and feel your age is against you it's time to get a mindset shift. There are numerous ways to maintain a positive approach to increasing age. Here are just a few examples:

1.) Start collecting evidence of positive aging. Compile an inspirational mid-life file and add clippings, photos, quotes, and 'case studies' of people who have made it big, or are happy at work, in their twilight years. Look for your role models. Gather at least 10 examples of successful people in your age group and above. You'll see a few of my favorite examples in the page that follow.

2.) Create an image board or journal. Paste inspirational quotes, pictures, and clippings which celebrate maturity in the workforce and life. Motivate yourself by adding to it and looking at it regularly.

3.) Turn age into an asset. Don't be disheartened by people who think your age is against you. Write down a list of the benefits of hiring a mature worker. Widen your awareness of the positives by asking others to add their views. Armed with your own self-belief and a few powerful strategies to market yourself, you'll be unstoppable.

4.) Network with other like-minded people. Talk to other mature job seekers, check helpful websites, and network with organizations that provide tips and examples to help you succeed and stay positive.

5.) Get career fit. Learn a new skill or get up to date with new technology that will help you gain the job you want. You're never too old to learn, and you may even discover a new talent.

6.) Rekindle a sense of adventure. Re-awaken dormant creative skills and adopt a playful approach to life. Take on some FTEs – first-time experiences. Can you think of anything you'd love to try? Like Carla Coulson, who in her 40's gave photography a go, found a new passion and has now made it a rewarding career.

7.) Challenge your assumptions. Divide a page into half. List any negative assumptions you might have about your age and on the other side write some counter statements. Here's an example to get you started:

NEGATIVE ASSUMPTIONS

Employers prefer younger workers

AFFIRMING Counter Statements

Demographic research shows that companies are going to need to recruit from a more mature labor pool

"THERE IS no substitute for bravery, creative thinking, and imagination if you want a rewarding career."
~ Peter Biggs, Former CEO of Creative New Zealand

Plenty Of Time To Make It Big

The encouraging news, according to some experts, is that life begins in the late 40's. Evidence suggests that many people don't reach their potential until well into their 50s and 60s.

American grandfather of motivational books, Napoleon Hill, whose best-selling book, *Think and Grow Rich*, was published for the first time in 1937, discovered from an analysis of more than 25,000 people that those who succeed seldom do before the age of 40, and usually do not strike their real pace until well beyond their 50's.

This data should be encouraging for those who 'fail to arrive' before 50 and offers compelling evidence that people should approach the mid-years with hope and anticipation!

IT'S NEVER TOO LATE

HERE ARE JUST a few people who have achieved success in their later years:

1) AUTHOR HELEN HOOVER SANTMYER was 88-years-young when her book *And Ladies of the Club* was published. It stayed on the New York Times Best-sellers list for eight months. It was her first novel in 50 years.

2) A FAILURE AT 65, Colonel Sanders was world-famous and wealthy at 80. His father was a miner and his mother worked in a shirt factory. Harland Sanders had to give up school in the sixth grade because he was so poor.

HE EVENTUALLY OPENED a small home-town restaurant in the Kentucky hills. All looked well until the highway was rerouted and he lost everything. He was 65 at the time and faced with a future barely surviving on social security, his motivation to try again kicked in.

"MY GOVERNMENT IS GOING to give me a hundred and five dollars so I can eke out an existence. Surely there is something I can do for myself and other people."

TAPPING into powerfully creative questions like this unlocked the key to what would be his major success—his mother's secret chicken recipe.

TURNED down by numerous restaurants at the time he turned potential failure into another inspired idea—franchises. It was an instantaneous hit, and the rest is history!

3) FIFTY-FIVE-YEAR-OLD RHONDA BYRNE'S life was at an all-time low. Twice divorced, her father had just died and her career was in crisis.

THAT WAS UNTIL, acting on an inspired thought, she created the DVD The Secret and later produced a book, both of which went on to become some of the biggest-selling self-help resources of all time.

AT THE HEART of Rhonda's inspirational series of products and resources is the law of attraction.

"EVERYTHING in your life is attracted to you by what you are thinking," Rhonda says. "You are like a human transmission tower, transmitting a frequency with your thoughts. **If you want to change anything in your life, change the frequency by changing your thoughts**."

Action Questions: How Can You Think Positively?

Take a leaf from Rhonda's secret to success and change any stinkin' thinkin' that may be lingering. Answering the following questions may help:

1. What results are you currently experiencing that you would like to change?

2. What thoughts would you need to change?

3. What thoughts would remain the same?

4. What things have supported you in maintaining a positive state of mind in the past? How could they be helpful now?

5. Can you think of some other strategies to help you keep your mind on what you want and off what you don't want?

*"We all have **big changes in our lives that are more or less a second chance.**"* ~ Harrison Ford, Actor

Client Success Story: From Unemployed to Franchise Manager

Aged 48, Ngaire returned to New Zealand after running a business in outback Australia. Things had not gone well after an economic downturn in the rural economy and she walked away from her business. Ngaire tried her hand at a few other things but realized there were few prospects for her in Australia so came home.

She returned penniless and alone with no work prospects. She was unsure if her skills were suitable for more modern careers, and initially thought about learning computer skills.

However, a friend encouraged her to read this book and work through a career coaching process. This helped her recognize and value her experience and realize how her current skills could transfer into other jobs.

Ngaire had always walked easily into work because she had lived in a town where everyone knew her and there was plenty of work.

After learning how to value and communicate her transferable skills and experience she re-wrote her resume and was successful in getting a job as a shop manager for a national food franchise. Her new employer valued her prior experience, maturity and management potential.

Ngaire achieved great success in her role and turned around many problem stores. She was quickly promoted and given more responsibility. Her pay packet received a nice boost too!

It takes courage and strength of character to leave a situation and start over again. Ngaire's secret to success was drive, determination and a solid work ethic.

Initially despondent and fearful, she is now happy, confident and not worried about her future. Ngaire realizes that there are more opportunities out there and that she has the power to create her own luck and seize opportunities that come her way.

Her employer had the foresight to take on a mature person, and together they benefit in ways they hadn't foreseen.

ROBERT KIYOSAKI, multi-millionaire entrepreneur and author of *Rich Dad, Poor Dad*, is right when he says, "There is no one in your way except you and your doubts about you. It is easy to stay the same. It is not easy to change. Most people choose to stay the same all their lives. If you take on your self-doubt and your laziness you will find the door to your freedom."

A Time Of Renewal

You are as old as you choose to feel. I know many people in their 70's and 80's who are still leading active work lives and enjoying a more healthier existence as a result.

"If you retire you expire," says 88-year-old Boyd Klap who vows never to stop contributing.

Check out this video (https://vimeo.com/122707475) and watch the value of being mutually inspired and inspiring, and of maintaining a spirit of curiosity through and beyond your middle ages. You'll see Mandy Scott-Mackie who had just embarked on a mid-life career adventure in outback Australia and hear Boyd Klap who tried retiring many times and got bored! I apologize for the sound quality—Wellington's infamous wind got the better of us.

Action Task! Visualize Your Future

For some, getting older can herald more opportunities. While for others, especially those without a nest egg, or a working partner to fall back on, seeking help to reinvent their lives and careers is critical.

WHATEVER SITUATION you find yourself in, going with the flow and waiting for life to 'happen' won't provide the emotional and financial security you seek. Actively plan for your preferred future, because that's where you're going to be spending the rest of your life.

The following sensory visualization exercise will not only help you clarify your preferred future, but it will also help you power up your subconscious mind:

1) DRAW A TIMELINE and put yourself on it.

Project yourself toward your preferred future – 10, 15, or 20 years from now. How old will you be? Note this down. Now create your ideal life in your mind's eye. Engage all your senses and record your responses to the following questions (try visually displaying your responses on an image or dream board).

WHAT SIGHTS ARE AROUND YOU? Are you surrounded by people who love you, or enjoying the solitude of nature? Are you living overseas in an elegant, romantic, calm environment or are you somewhere more high energy, bustling and commercial? What colors and things surround you? What do you see?

WHAT CAN YOU HEAR—THE peacefulness of the country, cries of acclaim for something you have done, laughter, live music, bird-song or something else?

WHAT SMELLS FILL THE AIR? The smell of your partner's cologne, or perfume as you work from home? The sweet aromatic smell of freshly picked grapes from your vineyard? What does your preferred future smell like to you?

HOW DOES your preferred future feel? Is it like the warm, smooth earth surrounding the lifestyle home where you live and work? The silky coats of the horses you train? The fine linen of your business suit, or the smooth denim of your jeans as your turn up to deliver a seminar? Notice all the textures that surround you.

HOW DOES your ideal life taste? Are you enjoying the foods from your organic garden? Fine cuisine on your overseas travels? Amazing meals out dining with clients as you travel the world? Or something else

BY VISUALIZING your preferred future and engaging your senses you have taken the first step in making your dreams your reality.

2) WHAT'S STOPPING you from living your dream now?

Note these things down, but resist the feeling of being stuck by actively willing your mind to create solutions. Ask generative questions like: How can I make my dream real? Where can I get help? How can I make a change?

Look back along your timeline and think about all the steps you would have to do to make things happen.

Who would you need to talk to? What information would you need to know? What finance would you need to acquire? How can you acquire it? What training or new skills would you need?

3) ON YOUR timeline begin to map out the stepping stones to your success and do something every day, no matter how small, to move you closer to your dream.

Don't worry if you don't have all the answers. This is only the beginning of your career adventure. The rest of the exercises in this book will help you fill in any gaps.

Preparing For Success

There is only one security in this life—the ability to manage change. Below are a few strategies to help you prepare for a successful change:

1.) Increase your self-awareness. "Pause for a cup of tea, David Lange, former Prime Minister of New Zealand once said, when people were rushing prematurely into critical decision-making that affected the country's future. Increase your self-awareness. Take time out to clarify what it is that you really want—and why. How can we have a knowledge economy if we lack self-knowledge? Listen to my interview on Radio New Zealand about this and other issues related to changing careers —http://www.cassandragaisford.com/media.

2.) Play. Approach the career planning process with an adventurous, curious spirit. In the early stages remind yourself that you are exploring. Deciding can come later. Nurture and encourage curiosity and allow yourself to dream. Ask yourself, "what if…"

It's also interesting to note the increasing emphasis being given to adults now to embrace their inner, fearless child. Tap into the 'kidult' trend to help with modern day challenges, advocate a range of experts, and work towards an idealized world, free of restraint. You may just surprise yourself.

3.) Spend time researching your options and generating alternative possibilities. Actively challenge any assumptions that may be holding you back.

4.) Affirm the positive. Keep your mind on what you do want and off what you don't. Your truest beliefs become your thoughts, your deepest thoughts become your words, your spoken and unspoken words become your actions, your concrete actions become your habits, your conscious and unconscious habits become your values and your values become your destiny.

5.) Get inspired! Surround yourself with all the things that give you joy. Sidestep the things that give you stress and look after your health so you have energy to make changes.

6.) Plan for success and set yourself free. Know when it's time to stop thinking about changing and time to take concrete steps toward your preferred future.

Work through the exercises in this book and buddy up with someone who believes in the beauty of your dreams and can help you stay on track.

Client Success Story: From IT Account Manager to Travel Agent

Bill Kwan's wake-up call happened in his 40s when increasing stress levels made a career move not just a nice thing to do, but a necessity. As his wife said, "If you don't leave now it will kill you."

Some people may have taken the easier option by taking stress leave or an extended holiday, but Bill chose to take a career leap and shift from a senior account management role with an international IT company to work in an area that had always interested him —travel.

He initially worked as a travel consultant for a local travel agency. However, changing careers did come at a price.

"I didn't just take a salary drop—it was a salary plummet," he says. However, what he sacrificed in salary was made up for in personal fulfillment. "I gained more time to spend with my wife and daughter, play golf and work in an area that I love."

"FOLLOW YOUR DESIRE, but make sure you plan for success," Bill says.

Bill already had his eye on his longer-term goal when he accepted the junior role as a travel agent. Two years after making his first move he purchased his own agency.

"OFTEN PEOPLE TRY to live their lives backwards: they try to have more things, or more money, in order to do more of what they want so they will be happier. The way it actually works is the reverse. You must first be who you really are, then do what you really need to do, in order to have what you want."
~ **Margaret Young, Author**

What You've Learned So Far

- Times have changed and age is now on the side for the baby boomer generation as skills shortages begin to bite and demographic shifts mean there are fewer younger people in the labor force.
- Economic, demographic, social and technological changes have altered the career landscape. There is a

huge amount of opportunity for people wanting to reinvent their working lives.

- The greatest challenge for mid-lifers is the willingness to embrace a sense of adventure and to think laterally and creatively about career possibilities.
- It's never too late to make it big—planning, passion, courage and positive views about aging are important catalysts to successful change.
- Nearly anything is possible—the mid-years are a wonderful time of renewal.
- Increasing your self-awareness, being inspired, dreaming about your preferred future and having a compelling vision are important parts of the change process.

WHAT'S NEXT?

Do you feel trapped in the same role you've always done? Do you have a sense that you could do anything if you only knew what it was. The following chapter will help you stretch your imagination, generate a range of possible career options and begin to take practical steps to reinvent your career.

3

IT ALL BEGINS WITH AN IDEA

"I PROPOSE A RADICAL, yet ancient notion: To build the life you want—complete with inner satisfaction, personal meaning, and rewards—create the work you love." ~ Marsha Sinetar, Author

MANY OF MY clients have said they could do anything if they only knew what it was. Finding the job of your dreams and standing out from the crowd begins with an idea, a dream or a hunch about what you would love to do and why.

However, this is not the way that many of us have been conditioned to think about careers.

Traditional methods used to choose careers like checklists and assessments are being transformed by some creative thinking. If you haven't listened to my interview on Radio New Zealand, check it out here—we're discussing this very thing.

Did you know that at the age of four, 96% of children think they can be anything they want to be, but by the age of 18 only 4% of them still believe it?

As people grow up, they tend to close down the sense of possibility and trade in their dreams for a steady paycheck and a proper job.

However, times are changing. An increasing awareness of the power of creativity is changing the way people choose jobs and careers.

For too long, the role of emotions has been left out of making decisions. After years of conditioning that work is something to be endured, not loved, it makes sense. But now these outmoded ways of thinking are being shed.

Thankfully now more than any time in the past, people have far more choice about the type of work they can do and where and how they do it.

As Nick Williams, author of *The Work You Were Born To Do*, shares in the foreword of this book, "Too few of us have been bought up to believe that it is possible to make our living doing something we love, that lights our hearts up and stirs our passions. This is what I call the work we were born to do, and is our true work. To find your true work is a great blessing, one of life's greatest blessings I believe. And to be paid for your work rather than work for pay is one of life's greatest joys."

ARE you ready to find your greatest joy?

THE EXERCISES in this chapter will help you free up your creativity and think more broadly about career options. They will also help you to bring into greater awareness your own criteria for job satisfaction. Remember to approach these exercises as an explorer.

The purpose is to help you think outside the square and to think laterally about possible career options. You do not have to make firm choices or commit to any action that you may not feel ready for.

You may not even feel you have enough information about yourself to complete the exercises. Don't worry. The main thing is to start the process of creating your dream role by planting the seeds of insight and inspiration.

Get Creative—Dream And Explore

Discovering your great joy and the work you were born to do requires allowing yourself to dream and explore. It requires tuning down the rational mind for a while and engaging the right side of your brain, and listening to your intuition and the stirrings of your heart.

Discovering your great joy and the work you were born to do requires a commitment and willingness to tap into your subconscious where unexpressed desires dwell. It requires allowing yourself to dream and imagine a reality that doesn't yet exist. It requires being creative.

To do this with work, you have to be prepared to challenge

current assumptions and allow yourself to dream about what could be possible.

"IMAGINATION IS MORE important than any other trait for my work and such an easy skill to develop. Never look where you think you should, the creation of a new idea is simply combining two or more existing concepts together. A new idea can be either unfamiliar, silly or both."
~ *Mark Olsen, Artist*

The Heart Of Creativity

Many people get caught up in the classical definitions of an artist when they think about creativity, but you don't have to be an artist, painter or sculptor to be creative. Imagining what doesn't yet exist and then bringing it into being lies at the heart of creativity.

The American Heritage Dictionary of the English Language defines the ability to create as: "*to make or cause to be or to become; bring into existence; pursue a creative activity; be engaged in a creative activity; invest with a new title, office, or rank; create by artistic means; create or manufacture a man-made product.*"

CREATIVITY IS ABOUT...

- Imagining what could be
- Dreams, hopes, and desires
- Challenging the status quo
- Being willing to change
- Thinking outside the square
- Drawing outside the lines

- Bringing something into existence
- Innovation and new ideas
- Taking risks, trials, and errors
- A wish for something better
- Tailoring for changing needs
- Uniqueness
- Producing something
- Designing new products and services.

Lighten Up!

Let go of needing to know all the answers, finding a cure for cancer, ending hunger, solving problems or creating the job you know for sure you will love.

Creativity, dreaming and exploring is simply a brain-dumping process that helps stimulate new ideas and connections. Start with an open, playful attitude—you can always get serious later.

Call to Action! Generating Ideas

Here are a few tips to help you unleash a sense of possibility and tap into your creative self. Jot some initial thoughts in response to the below and add further insights in your passion journal.

1) CLONE yourself

Imagine you've just been cloned. You are now five people! Each of you has gone in a completely different career direction. There are no constraints—money is not an issue. You can get any job you want and you're getting all the experience you need.

What would each person be doing or willing to try? Isolate and list the key elements that make each of the five careers listed below satisfying to each clone.

Carol a disillusioned counselor whose role was made redundant, wanted to get away from always hearing about people's problems. She came to me for coaching as she was finding it hard to identify roles which would excite her.

Before coaching, she wrote, "I'm starting to question whether I'm doing the right thing applying for jobs at the moment. It's stressful and I'm afraid I may end up in a role that I don't want. I'm feeling quite conflicted at the moment."

I thought the cloning exercise would be a great way to stimulate her sense of possibility and remind her of the things that gave her joy. Joy, one of my other clients reminded me recently, is the fruit of your spirit.

At first, Carol was skeptical. It all sounded very impractical. I encouraged her to let go of her rational mind and play with possibilities. Once we had a few ideas down, I reassured her, we could look at 'concrete' career options then.

Her clones included: being a financially successful global coach; a non-fiction writer; an artist traveling the world; a creative educator; and the creator of a thriving community.

We then isolated all the elements that made these roles fulfilling to each clone and stretched the boundaries further by exploring how these clones could combine into what I call a 'career combo'—a combination of careers strengthened by a core theme and united under one umbrella.

"I'm feeling excited," she said, as together we set about planning how she could make her career combo a reality.

If you identified a role that combines many jobs or have just invented a new job title, begin to think about where you could find a market or outlet for it. It may be that you do what I call a 'career combo'—a little bit of this and a little bit of that!

2) TAKE **what already exists and copy it.**

Much of what we have learned we copied from people close to us, like our parents, or teachers, before we put our own unique own stamp on it.

Who could you copy? Identify someone who is working in a field you feel you would enjoy and learn as much as possible about what they did to achieve success.

When I was stuck in a career trap I was inspired by the career counsellor who was helping me and I began to wonder, 'how could I do that?'

I looked at her skills and background and asked her what it would take to be like her, and what training she would or wouldn't recommend.

I then set out to forge my path in a similar way—even learning the interactive drawing therapy techniques I'd found so liberating when she first got me to draw that bird trapped in the cage yearning to fly.

3) TAKE **what already exists and modify it.**

'Job sculpting' is a technique from the Harvard Business School that involves tapping into the psychology of work satisfaction and matching people to jobs that allow their interests to be expressed.

How could you tailor your current role to increase the amount of time spent on activities that make you happy? If you are unemployed, how could you use the skills and experiences from your previous role to create your best-fit career?

4) TOTALLY REINVENT THE WHEEL.

How could you tap into economic, demographic and social changes to create a product or service that really excites you and for which there may be a future demand?

When Elizabeth Barbalich founded her successful company *Antipodes* she tuned into the growing interest in New Zealand products and natural skin care, free of animal testing.

"Designing is not the abstract power exercised by a genius. It is simply the arranging of how work shall be done." ~ W. R. Lethaby, Architect

Call to Action! Use Emotion Not Reason Alone

Human beings are fueled by emotion, not by reason. Studies have shown that when the emotional centers of our brains are damaged in some way we don't lose the ability to laugh or cry, we lose the ability to make decisions.

Harness the inspiring and motivational power of feelings by trying some of the following techniques:

1) Visualize your way to success. Some people have estimated that we have 80,000 thoughts a day and up to 80% of these are negative. Keep your mind on what you do want and off what you don't!

See your way to success. Create a mental image of what you want to accomplish or obtain by imagining the desired outcome in your mind. At the same time, repeat a positive, present-tense affirmation about your goal.

"If you want to be creative, stay in part a child, with the creativity and invention that characterizes children before they are deformed by adult society." ~ **Jean Piaget   Educational Psychologist**

Don't get stuck on the term 'visualization.' Different people have different dominant senses. The most common is the sense of sight. This is why for most people the process of visualization works well.

Others, however, may have a dominant sense of touch or hearing or smell. These people may have difficulty 'visualizing' but may be able to accurately imagine sounds, smells or feelings.

Work with whatever works for you but try to engage all the senses by imagining what you will see, what you will hear, what scents surround you, how surfaces feel, etc.

2) Create a dream board, passion journal or even a whole wall filled with images that inspire you and remind you of the things you want to manifest.

According to mind-mapping and creativity expert Tony Buzan, we think in images not words. Surround yourself with images that symbolize or reflect the things you want to create. Allow these images to inspire and excite you. Add a dose of color and engage all your senses.

I was clearing out some of my old journals one year when I came across something I had written back in 2000. "I will live in a house that is elevated with lots of sun and which is surrounded by trees. It will be elegant and streamlined, with simplicity at its core and feng-shuied to make sure it is the best it can be."

What amazed me was not what I had written but the astonishing realization that seven years later I was actually living in the house I had created in my imagination. I have done the same thing in my career.

'I dream I'm on vacation, it's the perfect career for me.' These lyrics from a song by the Eagles was a theme around which manifesting my perfect career centered. Clarifying my skills, values and interests provided further focus as did confirming my life purpose and the longer term goals I have for myself, my partner and my family.

We now live in a lifestyle property in The Bay Of Islands, in New Zealand—a popular holiday destination, working from home with clients all over the world. Sometimes when I'm coaching a client over the phone I walk around the garden. It's so much fun—work always feels like a vacation.

Gathering images of the ingredients of career satisfaction, including where I wanted to live and work, helped me see my way to career success and directed my job creation activities much more efficiently. Now that's powerful creativity!

It's also one of the principals of the Law of Attraction made infamous by the DVD *The Secret*. But guess what? There is no secret! What there is instead is a lack of conscious awareness about how to tap into the Law of Attraction to make your dreams and goals real.

You can make your goals holistic too, as I once did in my dream wall. The images reminded me about the importance of family, spirituality, relationships and longer-term life goals. They remind me of the importance of only doing work that allows me to balance my needs and to do work that is life-affirming.

The importance of thinking holistically will help you affirm your best-fit career—you'll know what other things are important to you when choosing or creating a career.

To learn more about this powerful technique watch me demonstrating it on television here >>

3) MAINTAIN THE FAITH! Stay positive and keep away from cynics. Tap into the awesome power of meditation, yoga and a spiritual faith-based perspective to help you maintain a positive expectancy, manage stress and increase your intuitive, creative powers.

Julia Cameron, an active artist and author of *The Artist's Way* and another thirty or so fiction and non-fiction books, advocates relinquishing too much effort and turning energy instead from one of stressful striving, to cultivating faith and trust.

Prayer, gratitude, acceptance and unwavering belief that everything happens for a reason, are just some of the many strategies she encourages people to embrace.

If faith is something you'd like to cultivate, you'll find them throughout the Career Rescue series. You may like to check out Julia's book *Faith and Will* or find your own sources.

4) ASSOCIATE ONLY WITH POSITIVE, success-oriented people. Get around winners. Fly with the eagles. You can't fly with the eagles if you keep scratching with the turkeys. Get away from the go-nowhere types and above all stay away from negative people.

If you've got a negative boss, or are surrounded by toxic co-workers seriously consider changing jobs. Associating on a regular basis with negative people zaps your energy and can condemn you to a life of dissatisfaction and underachievement.

Who inspires you? Add pictures of inspirational people to your image board or journal.

5) BE PREPARED to do the hard yards. Pursuing your dreams isn't always easy—if it was, more people would be doing it. What are you prepared to give up in order to achieve your desires? Free time? Money? Short-term pain? TV? Facebook? Laziness? Comfort? Guarantees?

How will you feel when you have achieved your dreams? Remind yourself of these feelings regularly.

6) TRUST YOUR GUT! As Einstein once said, "The intuitive mind is a sacred gift and the rational mind is a faithful servant. We have created a society that honors the servant and has forgotten the gift."

Allow your intuition to guide you to the higher ground as Oprah does: "My business skills have come from being guided by my higher self or my intuition. I am who I am today because of... intuition, my ability to feel what is right for me and allowing that to be the strongest guide in my life. Intuition is akin to God. It is akin to being led by that which is greater than yourself. My intuition, my intention and my passion have allowed me to be who I am and will take me to higher ground..."

Everyone is intuitive—many of us have just forgotten how to listen. As a life and career coach and holistic, energy psychologist I've always believed deep down my clients have always known what they wanted to do with their life.

Often what was missing was the courage to listen and then take confident steps toward their dreams. Intuitively I always 'knew' I could create a career that felt like a vacation. Initially, rationally I had no idea how, but I made it my mission to find the answers.

Listen to life's whispers and act on your intuition. What is your intuition telling you to do, be or have?

"A HUNCH IS creativity trying to tell you something." ~ **Frank Capra, Film-maker**

Action Questions: Dare to Dream

As author George Bernard Shaw once said, "Imagination is the beginning of creation. You imagine what you desire, you will what you imagine, and at last, you create what you will."

Try answering the following questions to unlock some of your dreams, and bring into being all the things you yearn for:

- What have you always wanted to do but never thought you could?
- What would you do if you knew you couldn't fail?
- When you were a child what did you dream you would be when you grew up?

"IT'S NOT your work to make anything happen. It's your work to dream it and let it happen. Law of Attraction will make it happen. In your joy, you create something, and then you maintain your vibrational harmony with it, and the Universe must find a way to bring it about. That's the promise of the Law of Attraction." ~ Abraham Hicks, Author

8) BUILD IT. Take a leaf from professional architects and build a model of your ideal job. Play with some ideas starting from the ground up. Create your ideal office space in every aspect, including the furnishings, people, setting (home or big city , etc.). If you can't build your ideal job physically, sketch it or create a 'story board.'

9) ACT AS IF. Take a job idea you are considering, or have always wondered what it would be like, and act as if you are doing that role. Dress the part and tell people about what you want to do as though you are already doing it.

ONE OF MY clients was struggling to get into a new industry due to lack of experience. I encouraged him to get out of his track pants and dress as though he was already a media and communications expert. I also suggested he have a business card designed that announced his desired job title perfectly. He also changed his voice-mail. Now instead of, "Hi, Rob here—leave a message," callers were greeted with, "Hello, you've reached Rob Murray, Communications and Media Consultant…"

Soon enough fantasy caught up with reality and he is now doing the job he dreamed of. Another option is to shadow someone who is in the role you are considering to get a feel for what it's like.

"BE the change you want to see." ~ Mahatma Gandhi, Leader

10) **BE PROVOCATIVE!** Provocation is a favored technique of creative guru and best-selling author Edward De Bono. It involves putting forward ideas you think are absurd in order to move your thinking forward.

Sometimes when you allow yourself to think of the most ridiculous, wild ideas you free yourself from constraints.

WHAT IF…

I REMEMBER RUNNING a career workshop in a large government organization and getting workshop participants to do the cloning exercise described earlier. One guy clearly thought this was a ridiculous idea, and just to prove that there was no way the exercise would be useful he wrote down that one of his clones would be an SIS agent.

"There's no way that will happen," he scoffed. Well, he nearly fell over when someone next to him said he had seen them advertising for agents in the paper that morning!

When you think about your next job, what are some of the most absurd or ridiculous things you can think of? Record your ideas in your passion journal. Are they really so absurd? Do any excite you? How could you make any of them a reality?

The Picture of Success: From Computer Sales to Renown Artist

A former computer salesman, Mark Olsen's creative bent emerged while dining at a restaurant one year. "I saw some paintings on the wall and said to my wife, I could do better than that."

So he set out to achieve just that. The first attempts were shocking, he confesses. But undeterred and fueled with a newly found passion to create he set about learning as much as he could about the art of creativity.

Primarily self-taught Mark made a determined effort to perfect his art. He spent time reading up on the process and studying the styles of other artists he admired. De-stressing by spending time in his personal flotation chamber (a light- and sound-proof tank filled with water) provided further inspiration.

Copycatting his way to success by studying the styles of his three favorite artists (Picasso, Modigliani and William Dobell) Mark blended the three to come up with his own unique style.

He enjoyed the process so much that he decided he wanted to make it a full-time career. "There was no question I was going to be this poor, stricken artist. I have no desire to live on the bones of my arse," he said.

Mark created a strong picture of his preferred future by imagining himself 20 years from that moment as a 60-year-old experiencing huge success.

It was clear he wanted to be a household name with strong sales around the world. Realizing that without a plan his dream of artistic success would not happen, he studied best-selling artists and, applying a strong marketing approach, set out to create his own brand.

Mark didn't wait for the art world to come to him. He went to the art world. He set himself big challenging goals including an exhibition at a prestigious London gallery—aiming low and settling for less was never on his radar. As they say, if you don't ask you don't get and as luck would have it a sudden cancellation of an exhibition created a well-timed and very fortuitous opportunity for Mark to have a solo show. Sales were so good that Mark quit his job in IT and has been earning a living as a full-time artist ever since.

Ron Espkamp of Exhibitions Gallery says, "Mark is an inspiration both as an artist and as a person. He has in a very short period established himself not only as one of New Zealand's greatest portrait artists but as an artist to watch on the international stage. Mark's success and distinctive style of painting have been a culmination of his passion, self-belief, determination, thirst for knowledge and extremely strong work ethic."

The things Mark has learnt as an artist are applicable to many people wanting to create a new picture of success for their work and their lives. A few of these creative tips are below. You can see more on Mark's website: http://www.markolsen-artist.com/whativelearnt.html

- To think as big as I can, never wait for the right time
- Surround myself with people that support me, avoid those who don't
- Take action every day
- Start by being wrong and new ideas appear.

"YOUR POWER TO choose the direction of your life allows you to reinvent yourself, to change your future, and to powerfully influence the rest of creation." ~ Dr Stephen R Covey, Author

CREATIVE JOBS

One of my friends is a barrister, but he prefers to call himself "a thinker"—in this way recognizing the blend of creative and logical skills he brings to his role. Another man I know calls himself 'an encorporator'—he's an architect, teacher, designer—amongst many of the creative hats he wears in his roles.

Here are some other jobs where people's true creative instincts are encouraged to flourish within a commercial environment:

- Futurist
- Brand Manager
- Strategy Manager
- Director of Business Development
- Business Architect
- PR/Communications Manager
- Graphic Designer

- Interior Designer
- Social Media Planner
- Blogger
- Change Consultant
- Product designer
- App Developer
- Entrepreneur/small business owner
- Life Coach

NATURALLY, this is not an exhaustive list. Can you think of any others that you'd like to explore?

ONLINE CERTIFICATION COURSE NOW AVAILABLE

Discover how to make money as a life coach, earn extra income on the side, and easily create your own online business using the Worklife Solutions fail-proof system & attract your first paying client in weeks. All from the comfort of your own home or exotic destination.

Navigate to https://the-coaching-lab.teachable.com/p/worklife-solutions-coach-training-foundation-course

Call to Action! Keep A Look Out

If a creative role appeals to you keep an eye on future trends and look out for jobs and organizations where creativity and innovation are core role requirements. Or do as I once did, either find an organization you'd like to work for and create a role for them; or employ yourself and start your own business.

IDEAS ARE **big business**

YOUR ABILITY and willingness to think outside the square is a highly marketable skill. It's not just the standard creative industries, like the movies and the arts that are tapping into creativity.

As international competition continues to increase, organizations are always looking for people who can help them innovate, read trends, and stay ahead of their competitors. This person could be you!

What You've Learned So Far

- It all begins with an idea when it comes to creating more happiness in work and in life.
- Many people confess that they don't know what they want and where to begin when it comes to getting more happiness at work.
- Leveraging off the power of creativity is a great place to start, and essential in this modern age. Many of the jobs that exist now will be redundant in the future, and future jobs are yet to be created.
- An increasing awareness of the power of creativity is transforming the way people choose jobs and careers.
- Regaining the sense of possibility and adventure that we had as children is an essential part of awakening desire, creating a picture of success for the future and making concrete plans of achievement.
- Discovering what you want means devoting time to dream and explore first. It means listening to your heart and honoring your intuition. It means being creative.

- Everyone has the potential to be creative. Creativity is simply the ability to bring something into existence. It's a skill, like any other, that can be acquired and perfected.
- Open-mindedness and a willingness to question the unquestionable is an essential part of generating new possibilities.
- True creativity stems from, and flames, the embers of desire—it's emotionally charged. Everything begins with an idea. Let go of rational, linear thinking and dare to dream. Let your imagination soar.

"All successful men and women are big dreamers. They imagine what their future could be, ideal in every respect, and then they work every day toward their distant vision, that goal or purpose."
~ Brian Tracy, Motivational Guru

WHAT'S NEXT?

Many people undervalue their skills and talents and forget to look for roles that enable them to both employ their strengths but which also enable them to develop new ones. The following chapter will help you pay attention to what you love.

4

VALUING NATURAL KNACKS AND TALENTS

"If you don't pay attention to what you love, you could overlook your greatest gifts! That love is the sure-fire indicator of hidden gifts, and it is the only way to find them. Skills don't count. They're just abilities that were useful enough to be developed. Gifts often haven't had the chance to be developed and because of that we're fooled into thinking they don't exist."

~ Barbara Sher, Author

PEOPLE OFTEN THINK that unless they have received formal training or gained experience on the job, or have a piece of paper like a degree, then they don't have any skills.

This is not true! The world is full of people who have achieved great things without formal training. Sometimes the best course of study is to teach yourself.

How many times have you heard of people who gained a qualification and were then told they lacked practical experience, or that they had to go and unlearn everything an academic institution had taught them?

I'm not knocking formal training. And in some professions, it's essential. But not all career paths require certification, or on the job experience.

No training required!

Van Gogh was a self-taught artist. He used his passion and natural ability with color and creativity to paint wonderful masterpieces that send hearts racing and are worth millions of dollars today.

From an early age, my brother Hadyn was wheeling and dealing. He has not done an MBA or had any formal training in business. Instead, he uses his natural entrepreneurial skills to create many successful business ventures. He tried going to University but quit because he felt academics were out of touch with reality.

As a child, my daughter Hannah has always had a strong connection to Spirit. Now in her late twenties, she has chosen to her embrace her gifts and has started a career as an intuitive life coach and spiritual medium.

A client of mine trained as a textile designer and, despite a lack of formal training in kitchen design, has successfully combined her passion for beautiful design, and her natural creative ability, into a successful career as an award-winning kitchen designer.

My mother has done the same thing, quitting a job she hated as a legal conveyancer in her 50's, then—after buying into a franchise, she set up her own shop as an interior designer—all with no formal training. A passion for design, a natural talent for creating beauty, a gift for knowing what looks good, and how to market her services, and loving making her clients happy, have seen her become very successful.

Now in her 70's, she's shut her physical store and runs her business from the comfort and beauty of her home. I share more of her story and her practical strategies for building a beautiful business in Mid-Life Career Rescue: Employ Yourself.

THE TRUTH **About Skills**

"Although men are accused of not knowing their own weaknesses, yet perhaps few know their own strength. It is in men as in soils, where sometimes there is a vein of gold which the owner never knows of."
- Jonathon Swift, Satirist

THE COLLINS CONCISE Dictionary defines a skill as "demonstrating accomplishment."

It's that simple. Do what you do well, and communicate your achievements. If you can't do something you love well, up-skill. There are plenty of ways to do this. Online courses, self-help books, shadowing others—and of course, formal tuition, where needed.

Most often though, there are things you do very, very well. But so many people, mid-lifers, and women especially, tend to under-value the things that come easily to them.

Three Types of Skills

The Dictionary of Occupational Titles, a primary text in vocational literature, makes a distinction between three basic types of skills: work-content or technical skills; self-management skills; and functional-transferable skills.

WORK CONTENT SKILLS

Historically these have been how we've always thought of skills —something in which you have had specific training, or have received a qualification in, rather than a natural ability or life skill.

Whilst technical skills, and specialized knowledge and abilities (often gained through formal education or training) may be important for some occupations, it is essential not to over-inflate their importance.

SELF-MANAGEMENT SKILLS

Many hiring decisions are made on the basis of self-management skills, often referred to as personality traits and preferences. Recruitment firms often use trait-based psychometric assessments tools to determine your aptitude and ability for the job. But they're only one part of the equation, and there's a growing body of research which questions their validity.

Personally and professionally I've always valued preference-based personality assessment tools, and am a certified and qualified practitioner of the Myers Briggs Personality Preference Indicator(MBTI), for this reason.

I explain this more and provide examples in my book, *Mid-Life Career Rescue: What Makes You Happy*. In brief, I rate this tool because it assumes you are the expert in your life, that you know your preferences best, and that if you wish to change—you can. Trait-based tools assume you are what you are, and won't change. They also very often disempower people, by placing others in the role of expert.

TRANSFERABLE OR PORTABLE Skills

Your self-management skills, along with your natural knacks and talents are the portable skills that are easily transferred into other roles or career paths.

For example, you may have a natural ability for teaching. You may, or may not, have combined this ability with a formal qualification or on the job training. Regardless, this natural skill is highly portable.

Your strongest functional-transferable skills or 'natural knacks" and talents have often been a core theme in your self-expression throughout most of your life. For example: perhaps as a child, you may have been persuasive with your parents in extending your bedtime; sold the most raffle tickets for your school; talked your friends into joining activities that you wanted to do; and won a debating prize in college. Convincing is a major functional-transferable skill running through these experiences.

The importance of focusing on your functional transferable skills and self-management skills

While ultimately the strongest skills you have in each of these areas must feature in your career planning, it is important to focus on your transferable, portable skills and abilities. They are the key to entering, redirecting, or changing careers. They are the constant factors you can rely upon to make you marketable, no matter what changes you need or want to make in the types of projects you address or the types of working conditions you have as a context for your work.

Unlike Work Content/Technical Skills, which are role or career, specific, transferable skills may be employed in a wide range of incredibly varied directions. For example, if you have a natural knack and a passion for organizing things, you can market that in a whole host of projects and settings. Some careers that require "organizing skills", for example, include: Project Management, Events Management, Administration Support Officer, and Deployment Management etc.

Call to Action! Generate Ideas

Break down the skill of teaching. What does it involve? Sharing knowledge, passing on skills, something else?

Brainstorm or list all the possible ways people make a living from their skill of teaching. Build your list by using generative thinking skills, and open questions like, 'teach- what, where, why and how?'

If you get stuck do some research. I just entered, "what skills does a teacher have?" into Google and came across some very useful information, including a site devoted to helping people find a new life *after* teaching. The tips they provide are relevant not just to teaching—check it out here >>

To transfer in or out of a career you need to build greater awareness of, and be able to communicate to prospective employers, your relevant transferable skills. And, as the link I shared above confirms, action verbs not only do this, they'll make your future job applications, or self-employment branding efforts, 'pop.'

It's 'Just' What You Do

People often take their functional-transferable skills for granted because they come so naturally they don't think about them. Often your strengths are so much part of who you are and what you do that you under-value them and may not realize that what comes easily to you is an area or skillset where other people struggle.

How many times have you been complimented and say, "Oh, it's nothing. It's just what I do"?

It's not nothing. Natural talents which, combined with your enthusiasm, create your point of difference. They're pure gold.

As you've read above, Van Gogh had a natural knack for creativity. Hadyn had a natural knack for trading. But the unifying thread, shared by all successful people, is passion.

It's Your Time To Shine

Many people think that by the time they reach their mid-years knowing what they are good at should be easy. However, as I've highlighted many people tend to take themselves for granted. And an astounding amount of people have suffered from years of neglect and lack of positive feedback.

Combine this with cultural messaging of the past, that work is something to be endured, not enjoyed, makes affirming the positive absolutely vital. As does challenging the notion that it's arrogant to 'blow your own trumpet."

How will people know what you're good at if you don't know yourself, and you don't tell anyone?

What gives you joy? What do you love doing? What would you do for free? Answering these questions and noticing the times you feel excited, alive, or in love with doing or being something, are vital signs confirming you are on the path with heart.

Being good at something, without enjoying it, only leads to heartache, boredom, and resentment in the longer term. As one of my unhappy clients said recently, "They keep promoting me but does anyone ever ask me if I like what I do?"

Just like the artists who learn to paint with their feet and their mouths, with the motivation you can learn to master a skill you don't currently have. But without motivation, it can just feel like a painful thing to do.

Call to Action! Identify Your Favorite Skills and Talents

If you're struggling to identify your favorite skills and natural knacks and talents, the following lists of skills, grouped in related clusters, will help. This exercise involves three separate stages: rating your joy, ranking your skill and picking the favorite talents you want to use or develop in your career.

1) Do you feel joy, happiness or contentment? When completing this exercise first identify your 'joy factor.' How much enjoyment does using this skill give you? Is it a skill you're motivated to use?

Rate Your Joy Level. Using the skills categories which follow, rate them from 1-5 according to their joy level: 1 -low enjoyment and 5 - high enjoyment

This is an important step in finding a job you will love but one so many people ignore. Instead, they concentrate prematurely on ability, forgetting motivation altogether.

2) How skilled are you? Once you have identified your motivation, self-assess your level of skill or competency. Think about your skills in relation to your whole life, not just your work.

Rank your skill Level from A–C. A is a strength, B is you're competent, and C you lack skill. This may be because you've never had the opportunity to use this skill, or because you know it's a weakness or something you need to develop

Don't let your feelings about how much you dislike, or think you would dislike, the activity guide your assessment. A lack of compatibility with your interests, or a clash of values, for example, may be influencing your feelings.

Perhaps you're too hard on yourself. Bring some objectivity to this exercise. Assess your present level of skill by referring to feedback people have given you.

INTERPERSONAL SKILLS

- Gaining trust and respect of others/building relationships
- Relating to diverse people
- Being sensitive to people's needs and feelings/empathy
- Building teams
- Contributing effectively to teams
- Mediating/resolving conflicts/building consensus
- Networking/building relationships
- Perceiving intuitively (sense, show insight, and foresight)

COMMUNICATION SKILLS

- Listening effectively
- Writing concisely and persuasively
- Speaking persuasively
- Translating complex ideas into everyday language
- Giving helpful, constructive feedback
- Making effective presentations
- Having compelling sales approach/presentation
- Speaking to an audience
- Interviewing for information

- Marketing/selling
- Proofreading/editing (checking writing for proper usage and stylistic flair, making improvements)

LEADING/MANAGING SKILLS

- Developing and communicating a compelling vision
- Inspiring/motivating others/communicating persuasively
- Gaining trust of others
- Giving direction/coordinating/organizing others
- Thinking strategically
- Planning
- Working effectively under pressure/demanding deadlines
- Gaining co-operation of people you have no direct control of
- Making decisions
- Initiating change (exert influence on changing the status quo, bring about new directions)

DEVELOPING OTHERS/COACHING SKILLS

- Counseling, advising
- Coaching, training and teaching new skills and competencies
- Motivating others to achieve their goals
- Giving constructive feedback
- Mentoring

PLANNING AND ORGANIZING SKILLS

- Defining goals and objectives
- Prioritizing tasks and assignments
- Project/event management (schedule and develop projects or programs)
- Delegating effectively to make the best use of others' skills
- Integrating efforts of others
- Thinking ahead and contingency planning
- Coordinating events, handling logistics
- Monitoring (keeping track of the movement of data, people or things)
- Implementing (providing detailed follow-through or policies or plans)
- Expediting (speeding up production or services), troubleshooting problems, streamlining services)
- Classifying (grouping, categorizing, systemizing data, people or things)

TIME MANAGEMENT SKILLS

- Prioritizing to best meet customers'/organizations' needs
- Establishing achievable goals and objectives
- Balancing work and personal life
- Delegating
- Prioritizing

LEARNING AND PROFESSIONAL EXPERTISE

- Staying current
- Developing new skills and knowledge to remain at cutting edge
- Being regarded as an expert in your field
- Emotional intelligence
- Resilience/stress management

FINANCIAL   MANAGEMENT/COST   SENSITIVITY SKILLS

- Preparing budgets, computing costs, etc.
- Establishing cost controls
- Managing activities to stay within budget
- Increasing profitability by reducing overheads
- Budgeting, economizing, saving, stretching money or other resources
- Cash flow forecasting
- Taxation
- Estimating, appraising, costing
- Counting (tallying, calculating, computing quantities)

PROBLEM-SOLVING AND ANALYZING SKILLS

- Breaking things down logically

- Systematic thinking
- Finding facts and information
- Researching
- Evaluating (assessing, reviewing, critiquing feasibility or quality)
- Identifying and diagnosing to get to the root of a problem
- Developing innovative, effective solutions to complex problems

CREATIVE SKILLS

- Portraying images (sketching, drawing, computer graphics, illustrating, painting, or photographing)
- Lateral thinking
- Generating ideas (reflecting upon, conceiving, dreaming up, brainstorming, improving)
- Composing music (writing and arranging music for instruments or voice)
- Entertaining, performing (amusing, singing, dancing, acting, playing music)
- Visualizing (imagining possibilities, seeing in mind's eye)
- Designing (structuring new or innovative processes, programs, products or environments)
- Producing skilled crafts

THINKING SKILLS

- Seeing the 'big picture'
- Conceptualizing ideas, models, relationships
- Thinking strategically
- Integrating and synthesizing information from different sources
- Forward-thinking—anticipating future needs and requirements
- Establishing achievable objectives
- Creative/imaginative thinking

RESEARCHING/ANALYZING SKILLS

- Initiating projects, interventions, programs
- Making decisions and following through
- Taking personal responsibility for decisions
- Dealing with ambiguity
- Gathering information, doing research
- Attending to small details
- Interpreting underlying themes from complex information

INNOVATION/BUSINESS DEVELOPMENT SKILLS

- Identifying and capitalizing on opportunities
- Developing new products to meet emerging needs
- Actively seeking new opportunities
- Generating income

CUSTOMER/CLIENT SERVICE SKILLS

- Strong customer/client-service focus
- Making a real difference to customer/client (high impact)
- Building and maintaining relationships
- Being seen as a business partner

TECHNICAL SKILLS AND KNOWLEDGE

List any work-specific skills and qualifications you have, i.e., professional qualifications, degrees, technology or machinery etc. that you can use well.

3) WHAT ARE your favorite skills? Having completed the first two parts of this exercise, you'll have a clear picture of where your joy matches your skill level.

Now list your most motivated skills—both those you are already skilled at, and those you would like to develop.

These motivated skills form an important part of your criteria for job satisfaction. You may either chose a role that allows you to work with your strengths, or one which helps you develop skills you love but need an opportunity to develop.

This was my strategy when I took a role working for an Employee Assistance Program provider. I turned down other higher paying roles because, although the job paid $30K less, it met my values and my longer-term goal to work for myself.

It was a greenfield role—one that lacked constraints imposed by prior systems and ways of working. It gave me greater freedom and creative control. And I got the chance to develop and grow a business and learn all that entailed, from the safety and security of a salaried position.

My new employer also paid for me to complete my counseling qualification and allowed me time off work to complete the training. Because they already had an established client base, I was also able to build the necessary practical hours to gain my certification.

In addition, skills which once demotivated me, like budgeting and organizing, quickly became favorites when I realized how essential mastering them was to developing a successful business.

Client Success Story: From Housewife to Nursery Manager

Mary had been at home raising her children for 15 years. She was desperate to find paid employment but felt she had no skills and was afraid no one would ever hire her. She felt a skill was something you were trained to do and that you had a piece of paper to prove it.

Career coaching helped her identify that her natural knacks and talents such as planning, researching, writing, planting and cultivating, and creating things were skills and had a commercial value.

"I'd always ignored them and denied I had any ability. They were just something I could do and that came easily to me. Until I saw them as skills I couldn't value them."

Career coaching not only helped Mary gain greater awareness of her strengths but also how they transferred into a wide variety of occupations. She was also able to describe concrete examples of how she has used these skills to accomplish something and to communicate the value of her experience to an employer.

Now, free of self-doubt, she is feeling much more confident about her abilities.

She proactively contacted organizations she would like to work for and after an initial trial period was offered a role as a manager of a local plant center and nursery.

Call toAction! Discover Hidden Skills

If you'd like further confirmation of your natural knack and talents, or your confidence and self-belief could do with a boost, the following exercises may help.

1) Forage for examples. Gather clippings, articles, job advertisements, and feedback—anything that awakens awareness or reminds you of what you can, or could do well. Notice the times you say, "I could do that!" Surround yourself with images of things that trigger something for you.

2) What comes easily to you? Notice the natural knacks or gifts that are easiest for you. They can provide a good clue to the work-related strengths you are most passionate about.

3) What makes you proud? Looking back over your life, what have been your proudest moments? What skills did you draw upon to make those achievements happen?

4) Collect feedback. Keep a feedback journal or notebook and write down some positive things people have said about you. Drag out any helpful performance reviews. Even your old school reports can confirm areas of core strength. I'll go into this in more depth shortly.

5) Notice clues to passion. Notice the times when you're doing or experiencing something, and you catch yourself saying, "I love..." or you feel excited, alive or inspired. Write them down so you don't forget them. Add to this, "I could get more of this feeling by..."

Many people find it difficult to give examples of how they have used their skills—after all, we don't go around analyzing ourselves, and our actions on a daily basis. Collecting positive feedback that others have said about you provides an objective way to record and confirm your skills, passions, and areas of strength.

The best-selling author of *What Color is Your Parachute*, Richard Bolles, believes, as I do, that we are unable to truly realize our strengths without the insight provided by others.

Collecting feedback makes it possible to recognize and affirm strengths that you may have overlooked or discounted.

The power of collecting feedback is powerfully summed up by businesswoman, Barbara Koziarski, in Kay Douglas' book, *Living Out Loud: 22 Inspiring New Zealand Women Share their Wisdom*.

> *"I realized that I had been collecting evidence of failures, telling myself 'I can't do this because...' and sometimes they were old failure messages from the past.*
>
> *"To overcome my doubts and fears I started to look for and collect evidence of my success... sometimes people would come up to me and say, 'You really spoke to me. That touched me,' and I'd go home and write that down.*
>
> *"So I started to think that I was worthwhile because I had proof of it. And once I could shore myself up with the external proof I got better at not needing it."*

You may wish to keep your feedback in an inspirational feedback journal so that you can refer to it often throughout the career transition process. Include feedback you've received in the past by thinking back over your lifetime, from childhood through to the present, and recalling insights into your strengths that people have expressed to you.

Sources of feedback could include family, friends, clients, employers, co-workers, old school reports, performance reviews, thank you cards and emails, etc. Don't forget to update your feedback journal regularly.

You may only hear the 'negative feedback' and catch the volley of criticisms sometimes lobbed at you - so looking for, and recording, instances of positive feedback is a great counter strategy.

SURF THE NET

I've been keeping feedback in a special journal for years. Like Barbara, I'm a lot more believing of my abilities now and don't update it as regularly as I once did. But whenever I need a motivational boost, it's a nice book to read. Click here >>to see one of my older journals. (http://bit.ly/2zoHCKH)

Getting Below The Surface—What Employers Really Want

"You can teach someone new skills with minimum effort. The challenge comes when you try to change somebody's natural inclination."

Many employers are more concerned with "softer skills" and attributes that are less easily taught. Your chances of succeeding during a career transition are greater when you list and give examples of your passions, motives, interests, values, personality traits and attributes. The stuff beneath the tip of the iceberg!

Call To Action! Do What Makes You Tick

List all your ingredients of career satisfaction, motivated skills, strengths and areas for development.

Trawl through the Internet and Google types of careers pursued by people with similar preferences to you.

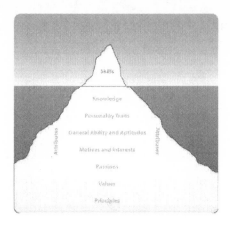

WHAT'S NEXT?

You've heard the call, you're feeling motivated to make a change for the better, and some excitement to get moving.

You've awakened your dreams, strengthened your ability to think laterally and creatively, and have some good ideas about what you would like to be doing career-wise. But that's only the beginning...

IT'S time to take a leap of faith and go for your dream. In the next section we'll dive deeper into specific job hunting and job search strategies.

PART II

GETTING THE JOB
YOU WANT

DEVELOPING A SELF-MARKETING PLAN

An effective job search campaign involves utilising the full range of job search strategies as well as focusing energy on the most important techniques—see the chart below for a summary of the most effective techniques. Some effective steps to help you prepare a job search marketing plan include:

- Identify target companies, roles and personal contacts who may be able to help—i.e. begin with the end in mind
- Identify strengths, areas of passion and ways you can add value
- Identify all the job search techniques and rate them according to effectiveness
- Prioritize time according to which technique is most effective eg networking is between 80-90 % effective so 80-90% of efforts should go there
- Identify all the steps needed to prepare an effective strategy, ie to network, some steps including identifying

all the people they know that may be helpful, identifying and researching prospective companies, etc; similarly for responding to the newspaper, steps may include emailing for a job description, researching the company, tailoring your CV, etc

- Keep track of marketing/job search efforts (ie who have they contacted, what follow up is required) and persevere... no, only means "not right now"
- Be patient but start early – an effective job search strategy often takes a minimum of 6 months

Job Search Strategy Effectiveness

A few statistics regarding the effectiveness for every 100 job seekers who try various job search methods follows:

RESEARCHING employers and approaching decision-maker through contacts

86%

Applying in person to an employer without doing homework

47%

Asking friends for job leads

34%

Asking family for job leads

27%

Using placement office at school/college once attended

21%

Responding to ads in newspapers (the higher the level of job, the less likely you are to be successful this way)

5-24%

Answering ads in trade journals in your field

7%

Employment Agencies (again, depending on the level)

5-24%

Mass mailings of resumes

8%

Computer matching services

4%

Source: **What Color Is Your Parachute?, by Richard Bolles and Job Seeking** *Methods Used by American Workers*, **U.S. Dept. of Labor, Bureau of Labor Statistics, Bulletin 1886.**

6

NETWORKING: DISCOVERING THE HIDDEN JOB MARKET

A bout 80% of all the positions available at any time are NEVER going to be advertised by Recruitment Consultants or directly by companies looking to employ someone.

By far the most successful job search technique is the process of networking—using personal contacts to uncover the "hidden" job market.

Largely this technique is so successful because organizations also use their networks to find employees when vacancies occur. Advertising is often a last resort, partly because of the time taken to screen applicants, but also because of the additional financial costs.

What is Networking?

When you need a builder what do you do? You ask a friend or an acquaintance if they know of anyone who's good. That's networking! We do it all the time; we just don't "label" it. Trust or lack of it is a key reason we don't rely on advertisements or the Yellow Pages. There are a lot of phoneys and crooks out there.

Networking is the process of accessing personal contacts via word of mouth to achieve a particular purpose. For the job seeker, this purpose is to tap into the hidden job market. For the employer, the purpose of networking is to find out if anybody knows of anyone that's a) good and b) available.

In its simplest form networking is often called "keeping an ear to the ground". Networking in the real world is nothing more than overcoming the fears of making contact with others. It's simply talk.

But it only happens through an orchestrated effort. You have to seek people out, get them to agree to meet with you, discuss your career aspirations and ask for more contacts. This is hard enough for some people to do face to face.

For so many that are new to Internet job seeking, it is nigh on impossible to do online. Or so it would seem.

BUT A GROWING CATEGORY of connecting tools are emerging online that will make job seeking-through-networking (or, Internetworking) not only easier—but essential in the years ahead.

REMEMBER, WORD OF MOUTH ADVERTISING IS ONE OF THE MOST EFFECTIVE MARKETING TOOLS!

If Networking Is So Effective why Don't the Majority of Job-Seekers do it?

FEAR! One of the most common reasons people don't network is because of fear of rejection or fear that others will think they are begging for a job. Lack of confidence and assertiveness are often other factors. Laziness can also sneak in– job hunting is hard work!

It is for these and other reasons that most job hunters prefer to use the more passive job search strategies such as:

- Looking in the newspaper, or on the Internet
- Registering their CV's online
- Approaching recruitment agencies

These strategies are passive because the job seeker is not taking control and out there actively hunting for a job. Instead, they are passively waiting for a job to come to them.

The Rule of Thumb is: DON'T PUT ALL YOUR EGGS IN ONE BASKET! Employing a variety of job search strategies is the key to success. If you rely on only the passive strategies you are missing out on 80% of the roles which either exist or which could be created for you.

Networking for Non-Networkers: A Guide to Feeling The Fear and Doing It Anyway!

Completing the following exercises will help equip you with the know-how to network effectively.

Remember this is the "active job-search strategy"—it does take energy and perseverance but the rewards are huge… finding the work you love, loving the work you found!

Call to Action! Prepare to Network Effectively

Some people have a negative mindset when it comes to networking. They think if they contact people they know that these people might think they are begging or hassling them.

Use your own words to describe the term "networking." Think about the benefits to the other person. Things like saving them the hassle of advertising for candidates if you happen to be a good fit for who they are looking for.

List some of the skills and personal attributes that are required to network effectively, eg research, persuasion, optimism, perseverance, confidence.

What skills and attributes do you already possess?

What skills and attributes will you need to develop?

Prioritize in order of importance. List some ways that you can develop and nurture the areas that are more challenging for you, eg affirmations, mentors, supportive friends, visualization, and self-help books.

The Aim of the Networking Meeting

Just like a fishing net, the aim of networking is to "catch" as much as possible. However, rather than fish, what the active job hunter seeks to gather is as many actual, or possible, job leads as possible.

The aim of the networking meeting is also predominantly about exploring information and gathering market research. This shift in focus from "give me a job" to "I'm interested in finding out about..." should help to minimize the fear of rejection and to take some of the pressure off all parties.

Remember: just as you don't like to be rejected, employers don't like rejecting you! The key things they are interested in "finding out" are:

- Whether your abilities, skills, and background match the employment needs in that business, industry, or organisation
- If so, whether any employment opportunities either currently exist, or are likely to in the future

- If not, whether the person you have initially contacted knows of people within their own network that may benefit from your skill-set and experience. Just like the Internet or World Wide Web – the objective of the active job hunter is covering as much distance as possible in the most effective way. Leveraging off the networks of other people is one of the most effective and efficient ways to do this.

YOU MAY STRIKE the jackpot and get a job, but if you don't, remember:

- Timing is everything
- Your aim is to generate at least two additional leads from each visit, email, or phone call you make.

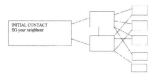

Identifying Your Network

This diagram can be very useful in identifying the groups of people that you know. It is by no means exhaustive!

(And you thought you didn't have anyone to network with!)

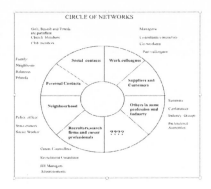

Call to Action: Getting Ready to Chat!

From the networking diagram, including any other potential contacts you have added, identify and prioritize five people you could approach and arrange an appointment to see:

HOT TIP!

You may wish to set networking goals for yourself to help keep you motivated—for example, 10 networking phone calls per week, resulting in 5 networking visits per week. Don't forget to include a reward for yourself when you successfully reach your goal.

Preparing for Success

Before you make your network approach you should:

Research the company and its senior people. Some of the things you need to be aware of and may need to be able to talk about include:

- Industry issues
- Organization structure

- Company products and services
- Industry and company profitability
- Competitors

REMEMBER: people like talking about their jobs and if your interest is based on soundly researched information you are providing yourself with an instant hook to gain their interest.

Cold Calls Versus Warm Calls

When deciding on your list of contacts to call remember to distinguish between "cold" contacts and those which are "warm" or "hot".

COLD CONTACTS ARE those you have never met, nor know of no one who can introduce you. After moving cities recently I approached the local health board to inquire about their services and to see if they may need mine as a holistic psychologist. I didn't know them and they didn't know me. Despite my spontaneous meeting and arriving unannounced the timing was perfect. They told me they were very short-staffed and my skills and experience appeared to be just what they needed. It's the old adage—if you don't ask, you won't get.

WARM CONTACTS ARE those who someone you know personally knows the person you wish to contact. In this case, your friend, for example, may be able to refer you or at least allow you to mention their name. This gets the relationship off to a warmer start than if you tried to establish contact with no prior "history' or connection.

Hᴏᴛ Cᴏɴᴛᴀᴄᴛꜱ ᴀʀᴇ those who you know personally. For example, I know the owner of our local bookstore. Recently he advertised for casual staff. Had I been interested in the role (I love books!) I would stand a 'hotter' chance of nabbing that job than someone 'cold' who walked off the street.

Rᴇᴍᴇᴍʙᴇʀ – even the best salespeople hate cold calling, mainly because the likelihood of "rejection" is increased ten-fold. Where ever possible leverage off existing relationships!

Making a Telephone Approach

Prepare! Prepare! Prepare! Every aspect of the job hunt process is about preparation—from writing your resume or CV, to preparing answers to questions that may be asked in an interview. Networking is no different especially when it comes time to pick up the phone and make that call.

You should have an outline script and responses to the most common objections prepared in advance. Remember that most people respond to appeals for help, so your call should use the phrase "help me" as often as possible.

You may wish to use the script which follows as a guide. It includes ways to respond to common objections.

It is important to remember that it is not so much what you say but how you say it that carries the most weight. Smile as you speak and, if possible, to stand—these both help you to sound more confident.

EXAMPLE SCRIPT:

CONTACT: "MARY McCRAE SPEAKING"

YOU: "Hello Mary, my name is John Farr. I believe that you are the best person to help me. Jake Evans from XYZ suggested that I give you a call. I am looking at the career prospects in the Communications/PR industry and Jake suggested that you are the best person to help me."

I wondered if I could talk to you about your industry before I make a move and would appreciate 15 minutes of your time."

WHAT FOLLOWS ARE sample responses to possible objections:

CONTACT: "I'm not sure I'm the right person."

YOU: "Jake spoke very highly of you and thought you would be the best person for me to talk to. I'd be really grateful for your advice - if you could spare 15 minutes."

CONTACT: "WE'RE not looking for anybody right now."

YOU: "I understand. Of course, I would like to get work inside the

Industry, but not right now. At present, I'm looking at opportunities in various areas and I need someone who could help me to find out more about your industry. Could we get together this week or next week?"

CONTACT: "I'm very busy right now."

YOU: "I appreciate that you're busy but I'd be really grateful for 15 minutes of your time. Perhaps I could buy you a coffee as a sign of my appreciation for giving up some of your time to help me."

CONTACT: "OK, NEXT WEEK THEN."

YOU: "Thank you. I really do appreciate it. Which day would suit you best and would you prefer morning or afternoon?"

(ALWAYS GO for non-core hours with late afternoon the best. Always offer to leave at the end of 15 minutes - most likely your offer will be refused in which case the obligation to close the meeting passes from you to the contact.)

The above example may seem repetitive and it is. It is important that you are persistent and don't lose sight of your goal—to meet with the person face-to-face.

YOU ARE unlikely to encounter all the objections listed, although you may get others.

Call to Action! Overcoming Possible Objections

Either list three of your most "feared" responses or those objections that you think or feel you are most likely to encounter.

The techniques for overcoming objections used in the example above were: Acknowledge the objection

- Restate your objective
- Use the "15 minute of your time" technique
- Offer alternative time/dates and always leave it up to the contact to decide which option suits them best

REFER back to the objections you highlighted and prepare some responses using the technique above. Record your answers. (If you couldn't think of any "objections" ask your friends etc for their input).

Questions to Ask When Networking and/or Breaking into a New Industry

Listed below are some typical and effective questions people use when networking or "interviewing for information". You may wish to adapt the ones below or to completely make up your own ones. It is helpful to practise asking these questions out loud until you feel comfortable asking them.

How DID you get into XXX, *eg Public Relations/ HR, etc*?

(People love to talk about themselves, and it's flattering to think someone is interested in what we do and how we got to where we are. This a great way to help build rapport and begin a relationship)

What advice would you give to someone wanting to get into the industry?

What do you see as the top 5 skills necessary to be effective now and in the future?

(This is a good question to check whether the skills you have now are valuable/marketable and to affirm areas you may need to develop in order to be successful)

What makes a successful (*Public Relations/ HR, etc.*) person?

What skills, attributes etc. do you look for in people you hire?

Why don't some people make it in this industry?

(This is a good way of finding out potential pitfalls and how you may highlight your strengths in areas where others may be weak)

What are the values of this organization?

What makes this a great place to work? What attracted you here?

WHAT KEEPS YOU HERE?

(ALL THE ABOVE questions are designed to find out the pros and cons of working within the specific organization you have targeted. Answers will confirm areas of "fit").

WHAT ISSUES IS **your organization likely to face over the next couple of years?**

(A good question to identify future skills needs and also to convey interest and enthusiasm in the organization's future. Helps to convey less of "What can you do for me?" and more of "What can I do for you?")

Closing Questions

Remember, the initial purposes of your meeting were to:

- Find out information
- See if there are any employment opportunities currently or in the near future
- Generate at least two additional leads

IF YOU HAVE ESTABLISHED good rapport and built a good relationship with the person you have just been "interviewing" they will be only too happy to refer you to other contacts they may have.

Remember this is how networking works and why it is so effective. You'd do the same, wouldn't you?

Most people hesitate when it comes to asking the sorts of questions below. Fear of "rejection" is a common reason why. Remember if you don't ask, you don't get. Besides most employers would be surprised, if not astounded, that you didn't ask—nine times out of 10 they will be expecting it.

If you are still reluctant or feeling nervous, you may like to think of a reward that you can give yourself when you "feel the fear" and do it anyway. Purchasing a new music album or item of clothing is a good reward. Each time you hear or wear it will remind yourself of the new, "courageous" you.

SOME CLOSING QUESTIONS

Do you have any openings now? If the answer is NO: Is this likely to change in the future?

Do you know of anyone else in the industry/this organization that it may be useful for me to talk to? OR

Do you know of anyone else in the industry/organization who may be looking for someone with my experience?

Ending on a Positive Note

You've heard that first impressions count—well so do last impressions! Be sure to leave on a positive, enthusiastic and grateful note.

You may like to conclude by using the example below or adapting your own:

"I really appreciate all the time you have given up to meet with me. I really like what I have heard. This sounds like a fantastic place to work/ like a fantastic role/career path. You must feel very lucky. Thanks again—I've gained a lot."

Key points to remember are:

- **Thank the person you have met**

Their time is valuable to them and there were probably half a dozen things they should have or could have been doing. People like to be appreciated.

- **Convey that you have really benefited from your meeting with them**

People like to feel that what they do makes a difference. Tell them what you have learned or gained as a result of their input. Your feedback to them is invaluable.

- **Show your enthusiasm**

The worse you can do is to leave the meeting looking unmotivated. Even if the meeting hasn't yielded the results you hoped for, remember the person you have just met may be your best advocate —advertising you by word of mouth to his/her own personal networks.

Follow Up

Out of sight does not necessarily have to be out of mind. Even well intentioned people forget—your job is to remind people that you exist.

Follow up one week after your initial meeting or phone conversation. Include a copy of your Resume or CV, if you had not already left this behind, and a thank you note.

THE THANK you note should include the following details:

- Confirm the date and time of the meeting
- Highlight key knowledge and insights you gained
- Bullet point how your skills and experiences fit the organization's current and future needs
- A "thank you" statement for the initial meeting and your interest in any opportunities that arise

When to Leave Your CV or Resume

Always have you CV with you in case an employer should ask to have a copy. It is also a useful "talking" document—while you are in your meeting you can point to your skills and experiences and talk about them in more specific detail than you may otherwise be able to.

The benefit of NOT leaving a CV at the first meeting is that you can further tailor it as a result of the new knowledge you gained. It also takes away the pressure you might feel about seeming like you are "begging for a job". We know you are not a beggar. You are an enquirer and an investigator—enquiring as to whether there are any employment opportunities and investigating what other opportunities might exist.

REMEMBER:

Everything that occurs in life is always a matter of timing. Be patient and have faith that when the timing and the situation is right the opportunity will appear.

Perseverance and maintaining a positive expectation is what separates successful people from unsuccessful people.

7

RECRUITMENT AGENCIES/CONSULTANTS

M any job seeker misunderstand the role of recruitment agencies and consultants. As a former recruitment agent for a large global consultancy here are a few "facts" to help you:

Recruitment Consultants are primarily concerned with the client's interests—they are there to help employers find employees NOT to help employees to find jobs. Their motivation is simple - $$$$$.

Employers pay them a fee upon successful placement of a new employee (between 10-18% of your salary). Realising they are not there to help you find a job will help you keep things in perspective.

If they do not have a job that fits, or they cannot see you as being particularly easy to place, you will not be a priority. Don't let this worry you. There are plenty of opportunities to be found else-where. Besides, as I have said, it doesn't pay to put all your eggs in one basket.

Consultancies and agencies do not cover the market comprehen-sively. There are many jobs that they will never hear about. Plus, one agency may have a preferred relationship with one company and have jobs listed that another agency knows nothing about.

How to Deal With Consultants Effectively

- When you contact a consultant, clearly state whether it is about an advertised job or a general enquiry.
- Be clear about your skill-set and what you are looking for – they are not there to help you work out what you want to do, or to help you think more laterally about career options.
- Telephone to follow up for an appointment – note that unless your CV is impressive or your skill-set is particularly relevant for a role they are currently trying to fill it is unlikely you will gain an interview. Once again, do not take this personally as a "rejection". Remember who pays their fees!
- Out of sight unfortunately often means out of mind. Consultants are ordinary people who are busy. Don't be dis-heartened if they do not return your calls – this is normal, unfortunately. Don't take it personally. Stay in touch and persevere. Even well intentioned people forget – your job is to remind the recruitment consultant that you exist.
- If you get an interview remember their job is to screen you for fit. Always aim to establish a mutual feeling of friendship and respect – but don't let your guard down.

RESPONDING TO ADVERTISEMENTS

A s I've shared in this book, only 20% of all the positions available at any time are going to be advertised by recruitment consultants or directly by companies looking to employ someone.

When reading an advertisement there are two categories that the required skills and experience fall into:

1. Essential (must have, critical, essential...)
2. Preferable (ideally, preferably...)

If you have all of the essential skills/experience and more than 40% of the preferable skills/experience, it is worth applying.

Recruitment consultants and search firms (the "Head-hunters") are client-driven, and are paid either on completion of an assignment or when given a brief. You mean $ to them only if they can place you in a position.

If you see an advertisement where either the company or the type of job interests you, but you do not have the experience or skills, it might be worth making a networking contact (once the rush of applicants has finished), to investigate how you might get in the field.

Which publications or Internet sites are likely to have recruitment advertisements relevant to you?

Responding to Advertisements

- Always write your letter on the basis of what you can **do** for the advertiser.
- Always tailor your replies to the information provided in the advertisement – go over the advertisement with a highlighter pen to remind yourself of what to cover in your letter.
- When responding by letter, feedback what you know the recipient of your letter wants to hear and no more. Be definite about being keen to apply. Point out that you meet all of the requirements (or nearly all)
- Avoid providing information that is not requested as you will only increase the risk of being screened out – remember the "15 seconds to impress" test
- If you are responding to an advertisement by telephone, be polite and eager, stating that you wish to apply for the position. Provide the minimum of information required to secure your appointment for an interview. Remember that getting an interview is your key objective.
- Avoid being interviewed on the telephone. Remember, you do not want to be screened out. However, if you get a positive response on the phone, see if you can arrange an appointment and take your CV with you.
- You will usually have to send your CV in at first contact.

Your covering letter is still of vital importance and should directly highlight your value to the advertising organisation.

- Remember that your CV and cover letter may become separated – do not run the risk of packing all the relevant information into your cover letter and failing to update/tailor your CV. Your CV should be capable of standing alone. This is especially important when dealing with recruitment firms who may scan your CV into their databases and discard your cover letter.

The Cover/ApplicationLetter

Suggested format

THE PURPOSE of this letter is to get the employer to read your CV or resume and invite you for an interview. Use this type of letter to respond to job advertisements and vacancy announcements.

Your approach here is to show that your qualifications fit the employer's requirements for the position. Analyse the position description carefully and pick out key phrases. Try to match your letter point by point to the requirements by emphasising key parts of your CV or resume.

WRITING style

Before writing your letter, analyse your reader by considering his/her requirements and needs. Plan your letter accordingly, placing the most important items first, supported by facts. By putting yourself in the reader's situation, you will better understand his/her needs.

After this analysis you can write a letter demonstrating how your background, training, work experience, and abilities can meet those needs. Such an approach will help you persuade the reader that you are a good match for the position and that he/she should interview you.

Remember that you are responsible for explicitly communicating your value to the employer. Do not expect employers who typically receive hundreds of letters for each job opening to wade through a great deal of text or a poorly written, mundane, or disorganized letter to figure out what you can do for them.

NOTE: *a cover letter should never replace your CV* **or resume. Many job seekers make the mistake of tailoring their cover letters but not their CV's. If in doubt your CV should take priority.**

THIS IS PARTICULARLY important with today's technological advances where many organisations are scanning CV's into their databases, which then use artificial intelligence to search for key words and then match relevant (tailored) CV's to positions they are seeking to fill.

Experienced letter writers follow these basic principles:

1. Take the time to research each employer's organisation and personalise each letter. Indicating that you know something about the company shows that you are careful and interested in the employer. This approach is much more effective than sending out hundreds of identical form letters.

2. Highlight one or two of your most significant

accomplishments or abilities to show you are an above-average candidate. Selecting only one or two special attributes helps your chances of being remembered. Be brief; demonstrate that you understand the value of the reader's time.

3. Use a polite, formal style that strikes a balance between confidence in yourself and respect for the employer. Be clear, objective, and persuasive rather than simply describing your background.

4. Be positive in tone, content, and expectations. Do not add details about yourself, your past experience, or your preparation that may call attention to your weaknesses or raise questions about your confidence or ability to do the job.

5. Use active voice and powerful action verbs in your writing to hold the reader's interest and convey a sense of energy.

6. Group similar items together in a paragraph; then organise paragraphs so that they relate to each other logically. Avoid writing that lumps together unrelated information without a strong topic sentence to tie the information together. Remember it is your responsibility to organize the information for the reader.

7. Always back up general statements with specific facts or examples. Documentation creates credibility and reduces uncertainty and abstraction for the reader.

8. Avoid jargon and clichés. It is tempting to use ready made phrases such as "self-starter," "proven leadership skills," "excellent interpersonal skills," etc, but using today's buzz words can suggest parroted formulas rather than original thought.

9. Check the spelling and grammar in all correspondence.

If you are not confident of your ability to detect grammatical, punctuation, or English usage errors or if you need help in organizing your letters, bring your correspondence to a professional for assistance.

10. Never misrepresent yourself by overstating your experience or skills. Even if you do not have every qualification sought by the employer, stick to the facts and tell the truth by emphasizing your strengths.

EXAMPLE 1 WHICH FOLLOWS, illustrates what to include in each part of the letter;

Example 2 is a standard letter of application.

While these assume you are mailing your application, you can after the text when you are attaching as an email, or copying and pasting into an online application.

EXAMPLE 1: Application Letter
Address
Date of Writing

Name
Title
Company
Street Address
City
Dear Mr/Ms
1st paragraph Explain why you are writing; identify the position and your source of information. Indicate in summary form

your strongest qualifications for the position using a series of phrases.

2nd paragraph Outline your strongest qualifications in more detail and show how they match the position requirements. As much as possible, provide evidence of your related work, extracurricular, and academic experiences and accomplishments. Refer to your enclosed CV.

3rd paragraph Optional. Convince the employer that you have the personal qualities and motivation to succeed. Relate your interests and qualities to your knowledge of the company.

4th paragraph Request an interview and indicate how and when you can be contacted. Suggest that you will call at a specific time to discuss interview possibilities. Thank the reader for his/her consideration.

Sincerely,

(Handwritten or electronic signature)

Your name, typed

Enclosure(s)

EXAMPLE 2: **Application Letter**

ADDRESS

DATE OF WRITING

Name

    Title

    Company

Street Address

City

Dear Mr/Ms... ,

I am applying for the Sales Associate position which was advertised in recently in The Dominion Post on (date). My varied sales experience and my bachelor's degree in Business Administration are my strongest qualifications for this position.

As you can see from the enclosed CV, I have sold a variety of products through my extracurricular activities and have worked in many banking environments throughout my career. My marketing, computer research, and customer relations experiences, as well as my oral and written communication skills, should prove valuable in increasing (name of company's) sales volume. I am enthusiastic about pursuing a career in sales with (name of company) because of its diverse product line and international scope.

I would welcome the opportunity to meet with you and can be reached at (phone number) from noon to five daily. I will be in New York next week and will call you on (date) to discuss the possibility of an interview.

SINCERELY,

(HANDWRITTEN SIGNATURE)

YOUR NAME, typed

Enclosure(s)

INTERNET JOB SEARCH STRATEGIES

Many employers have been quick to seize the benefits of on-line advertising when they have vacancies. These include global reach and continuous advertising.

For you the benefits include not having to leave your desk, and access to a wide variety of jobs. In addition some sites will email you with roles that may suit your criteria. Some of the major sites also provide CV templates and tips for job search and interviews.

If you are sending your resume or CV to these sites bear in mind:

You are one of the countless thousands on their databases, and hence you may have little success. You may find the traditional channels could have worked much better - ie paper documents and responding to newspaper advertisements. The key is don't rely on only this one job search strategy!

Some recruiters and large employers have scanning CV software so no human actually reads and vets it first. It gets scanned into the database and if your CV has the correct key words then your name should come up.

So with these tips in mind you are ready to go.

Check out some of these job search sites for those aged 50+

The following sites are geared toward helping you beat "age bias":

WHATSNEXT.COM

The What's Next job search site is your one-stop-shop. It has online assessment tools, career guides, loads of books and articles filled with expert advice, and links to career coaches—to help you figure out how to create the life you want in a career you want. The site is geared toward older workers and also has a Dream Blogs section where you can read real-life stories of the career changes that others have successfully made.

RETIREDBRAINS.COM

This job resource site was created by retired brains for retired brains. It provides quality information on finding temporary or seasonal jobs, as well as starting your own business, working from home, writing your CV or resume, finding full-time work, and continuing your education. And all the information is geared for the 55+ audience. Awesome!

RetirementJobs.com

You can post your resume here and search for full-time or part-time jobs online. Here's what the website has to say:

"Here at RetirementJobs.com, our goal is to identify companies most-suited to older workers and match them with active, productive, conscientious, mature adults seeking a job or project that matches their lifestyle."

WORKFORCE50.COM

Sign up for job alerts, check out the list of favorite age-friendly employers by industry, and apply for roles. (Previously known as SeniorJobBank).

MORE JOB SEARCH SITES:

https://www.monster.com/

This global recruitment portal can help you find the best jobs, coolest employers and career advice.

HTTP://WWW.JOBCAFE.CO.NZ

JobCafe is a site created for jobseekers, employers and recruiters to meet and market their skills and/or services.

It has an exceptional, state of the art, search system and has access to key career information which you can use, for free!

It's a great site to use if you which to meet talented job seekers, market your roles or profile your company. You can also use Jobcafe as a resource centre for recruiting tools such as personality and skills assessments.

HTTP://WWW.NZ.HUDSON.COM

Hudson is one of New Zealand's largest and most successful recruitment and human resource consulting firms.

HTTPS://WWW.YUDU.CO.NZ

Tell the world what YUDU (as in 'you do'). Create your online resume and set up a YUDU profile. Use it to apply for jobs and get yourself in front of the right people quickly and easily.

HTTP://WWW.SEEK.CO.NZ

This site allows you to either search the field of work you are interested in or scan the latest recruitment newspaper pages. *Seek* has a section devoted to IT jobs and a section for those wishing to work in the UK.

HTTP://WWW.NZHERALD.CO.NZ/EMPLOYMENT

This site contains career information and articles straight from the *New Zealand Herald*. Has a link to https://www.yudu.co.nz if you wish to search for jobs.

HTTPS://WWW.CAREERS.GOVT.NZ/

This site has an extensive database of jobs and job information to help you choose the right career. It offers you job advice, course and training information, career ideas trends, online tools and training.

HTTPS://WWW.KORNFERRY.COM/FUTURESTEP

This international professional search and recruitment company provides information on future career trends, top talent trends and assistance with finding roles.

Using Social Media To Find a Job

Chapter Nine: Networking: Discovering the Hidden Job Market highlighted the importance of taping into your social networks. The online community is an important aspect of this. Whether this is

Facebook, Instagram, Linkedin or something else, it's important to maintain a presence.

Recently I was in a writer's forum and a lady based in the States provided helpful information in response to a question I raised on Facebook. Later she offered her services and we corresponded for sometime. While I didn't hire her that time, I might in the future.

The important thing is that by maintaining your social networks and sharing your passion for what you do, you may just end up getting hired.

Studies have shown that 92 per cent of companies are using social media for hiring, including screening and vetting potential candidates.

Here are a few simple tips to help you use social media to find a job:

- Be authentic—use your real name and align your messaging with your values, passion and purpose
- Be professional—keep your image and content professional and consistent; avoid too much sharing of personal content which may be misinterpreted or cause offence. Be sure to an personal information is squeaky clean
- Use your social accounts as introduction points—it should link off to somewhere that people can learn more about you. On your social media accounts, be sure to include a link to the projects you've worked on and are currently working on. This may be a blog, vlog, landing page, online article about you, or somewhere else people can learn about you
- Streamline—being "active on social media" doesn't mean being on every platform. Understand your market and know where your audience hangs out. Some experts

suggest that every job seeker should have a LinkedIn account, beyond that, consider what's really important for your industry

- Brand You—If you want to stand out in a crowded market consider developing a compelling and easily recognisable brand. This may or may not involve a website. You want people to know who you are, what you do, what you can offer, and where you're heading
- Plan your social media strategy. Update your content regularly and devise a plan for how often you'll be interacting. Maintain some balance
- Be a thought leader—don't just share your own stuff. Situate yourself as an expert in your particular field. Share great articles or information of interest that supports your brand
- Follow job search experts—this will help keep your feeds updated, receive helpful advice, and boost your motivation
- Don't be shy. Be sure to mention your relevant social media links in your CV or resume

Lastly, but importantly, don't just interact with the hiring manager or recruitment personnel. Very often the most influential people when it comes to vetoing who gets hired and who doesn't are staff within the organization, or associated family and friends.

Don't forget to connect with people you may not know and also maintain a relevant presence in groups and forums. Very often it's not what you know, or who you know, but who you get to know that can herald career enriching fruit.

10

KEEPING TRACK OF APPLICATIONS

P utting your job search skills into practise takes careful planning and persistence.

The table below has been designed to help you keep track of your job search activities and to analyse each action in detail. Remember to include dates, names and other important "reminder"' details when completing.

ACTION	FOLLOW UP	BARRIER	REMEDIES	OUTCOME
eg CV sent, position description requested, phone conversation on xx/xx/xx	eg Phone Jo at recruiter XXX to check CV received	eg Jo not returning calls	eg Go to XXX and wait in reception	Jo has shortlisted me for position as ABC at organisation XYZ

ACTION
> FOLLOW UP
> BARRIER
> REMEDIES
> OUTCOME

BELOW IS AN EXAMPLE:

ACTION

CV sent, position description requested, phone conversation on xx/xx/xx

FOLLOW UP

Phoned Jo at recruiter XXX to check CV received

BARRIER

eg Jo not returning calls

REMEDIES

Go to XXX and wait in reception

OUTCOME

Jo has shortlisted me for position as ABC at organization XYZ

What's next?

TAKING care of yourself is another important, but often neglected, part of making a successful career change. Making changes, even positive ones, can send the stress levels soaring.

You may have been so unhappy in your previous role that you are already stressed out. Or perhaps the stress of being out of work for so long is beginning to take a toll.

The following chapter will help you get your groove back. Stress less and build greater stress resilience through the change process by working through the exercises which follow.

You'll also find loads and loads of helpful strategies in my book, Stress Less. Love Life More: How to Stop Worrying, Reduce Anxiety, Eliminate Negative Thinking and Find Happiness.

PART III

11

STRESS LESS

HAVE you been unhappy at work for so long that some of the symptoms of stress, such as feelings of depression, anxiety or even anger, are really entrenched?

Or is the idea of making a change causing you to feel anxious? Whatever your current situation there is no doubt that managing stress is a key component of making effective career decisions.

Stress is something we all feel everyday. It isn't something that only happens when we're under particular pressure. Some mild stress is good for you. It gives you a feeling of excitement and makes you want to strive to do better. It reminds you that you're alive, and it can help you thrive.

But too much stress can do the opposite. Stress overload can make you feel overwhelmed and empty, devoid of enthusiasm; or worse, of a will to live.

Negative thoughts and feelings are a classic sign of too much stress. It's hard to feel hopeful about the future when you are feeling down, overwhelmed or anxious.

So it's not surprising that it can be hard to believe in yourself, or to remember the things that make you happy. More often than not, during times of strain your self-esteem and confidence can take an awful hit.

Biologically we're incapable of sustaining prolonged levels of stress, no matter how great our will. If you don't address your stress, your body's adaptive resources can become exhausted—making you sick. Too much stress can give you chronic headaches, affect your blood pressure, contribute to depression and cause ulcers and heart disease.

Thankfully there are simple but powerful strategies at hand to help you avoid too much 'bad' stress, so you don't become ill, anxious or depressed during the change process.

And who knows, maybe once you have your stress levels back in check, or have found ways to proactively remove the sources of stress in either your work or private life, you may end up falling back in love with a job that you'd come to hate.

Heed The Early Warning Signs

According to a definition from The New Zealand Department of Occupational Safety and Health (OSH), stress is a reaction to the excess pressures you face in your life, and arises when you feel you can't cope.

This feeling of not being able to cope is an important point I will come back to, but one of the key things to remember is that worrying about not coping, even if it is not actively voiced, triggers the promotion of stress messages in your brain.

You may be so busy trying to juggle everything that you are unaware of how much strain you are under. Like Roger, who hates his career so much he says he hates his life. Or Jan, who can't relax, and is so busy being busy that she can't remember the last time she felt real joy.

The Biology Of Stress

When your life lacks balance this leads to a state of brain chemical imbalance known as —OVER STRESS. These negative brain messages then flow to other organs in your body sending them into overdrive and a high state of alert.

People who are overstressed complain of being tired but unable to fall asleep or enjoy a restful night's sleep. They have plagues of aches and pains, lack of energy, and can't remember what makes them feel truly happy. They feel depressed, anxious, tearful, snappy and irritable or just unable to cope with life.

Many people soldier on ignoring the signs their body is giving them. Some live to tell their stories and the lessons they learnt. As I've already said, I was so stressed and unhappy at work I got shingles. Others aren't so 'lucky.' One of my colleagues suffered a heart attack and later died.

Stress is an invisible killer, and the underlying cause of mental illness, depression and suicide. It's that serious—no wonder the onus on employers to help employees manage stress has been written into health and safety legislation. But don't rely on anyone else to be proactive about your well-being.

Listen To Your Body Barometer

The key to managing stress successfully is to heed the early warning signs. By nipping your stressors in the bud before they go to seed, you will avoid wreaking havoc with your body, mind and spirit.

You'll also avoid derailing your career and damaging your relationships. Increasing your coping skills can also be a wonder cure for dissatisfaction with your work, or your life.

"He who is of a calm and happy nature will hardly feel the pressure of age." ~ Plato

Signs and Symptoms

"Stress can cause severe health problems and in extreme cases, can cause death. Stress management techniques are conclusively shown to have a positive effect on reducing stress." ~ Mindtools.com

How stressed are you?

Take the following body barometer test by taking note of any symptoms you're currently experiencing.

PHYSICAL SIGNS **of stress**

- Increased heart rate
- Pounding heart
- Sweaty palms
- Elevated blood pressure
- Tightness of the chest, neck, jaw and back muscles
- Headache
- Diarrhea
- Constipation
- Unable to pass urine or incontinence
- Trembling
- Twitching
- Stuttering and other speech difficulties
- Nausea
- Vomiting
- Sleep disturbances
- Fatigue
- Being easily startled
- Shallow, rapid breathing
- Dryness of mouth or throat
- Cold hands
- Susceptibility to minor illnesses
- Itching
- Chronic pain
- Sore eyes

EMOTIONAL SIGNS **of stress**

- Tearful
- Impatience
- Frightened
- Moody
- Highs and lows
- Feeling of loss/grief
- Depression
- Anger
- Irritability
- Short-tempered
- Anxiety
- Rage
- Critical

COGNITIVE SIGNS **of stress**

- Forgetfulness
- Preoccupation
- Errors in judging distance/space
- Diminished or exaggerated fantasy life
- Reduced creativity
- Lack of concentration
- Diminished productivity
- Lack of attention to detail
- Orientation to the past
- Diminished reaction time
- Clumsiness
- Disorganization of thoughts
- Negative self-esteem

- Negative self-statements
- Diminished sense of meaning in life
- Lack of control/need for too much control
- Negative evaluation of experiences

BEHAVIORAL SIGNS **of stress**

- Carelessness
- Under-eating – leading to excessive weight loss
- Over-eating – leading to weight gain
- Aggressiveness
- Increased smoking/starting smoking
- Withdrawal
- Argumentative
- Increased alcohol or drug use
- Listlessness
- Hostility
- Accident prone
- Nervous laughter
- Compulsive behavior
- Impatience
- Agitation

SOCIAL SIGNS **of stress**

- Relationship difficulties

- Increased conflicts
- Marital issues
- Alienation/withdrawal
- Domestic violence

SPIRITUAL SIGNS of stress

- Hopelessness
- Doubting of values and beliefs
- Withdrawing from fellowship or group support
- Decreased spiritual practices (i.e. prayer, meditation, yoga etc)
- Becoming angry or bitter at a higher power or God
- Loss of compassion —for self and others

KEEP an eye out for any warning signs your body barometer may give you in the future. Proactive, not reactive, care is the best strategy.

"WHETHER OR NOT A PERSON EXPERIENCES STRESS AT work depends upon the person's perception of what is going on and the person's coping skills. It is not the circumstance, it is your REAC-TION to it that counts." ~ Dr Al Siebert, Author

Call To Action! Stress-Busting and Building Resilience

1) Identify what's stressing you out—stress is cumulative, and if it's prolonged, or we have too much on the go at once, our normal coping skills can be diminished.

Making a list of all the things that are worrying you or that stress you out, and then trying to work out solutions, is an effective way to get some control over your stress levels. Think possibilities not actualities to unlock creative ways of resolving issues.

2) TAKE CONTROL—REMEMBER it's not the event which is stressful but your reaction. You can beat the stress response by taking control of the things you can influence with things that are foreseeable. For example, Mary's boss used to stress her out because he always dumped things on her at the last moment. To reduce her stress levels she decided to proactively manage his diary, and she also called a meeting and told him she would work more effectively if she could have a greater lead time to prepare. He was glad she told him as he had no idea his behavior affected her in this way.

3) PREPARE—IDENTIFY stressful events in advance, and minimize the stressful situation—e.g., get up earlier to avoid running late; go to interviews for jobs you don't want so you can practise, and be less stressed and more skilled when the interview is for a job you really want.

You can also reduce your stress reactions by doing things that build resilience, i.e., if you know you have a heavy load coming up factor in more self-care activities, improving your diet, having a massage, meditating, relaxing or exercising, are just a few strategies.

4) PLAN YOUR DEFENCE—WHAT is the most realistic solution to your current situation? What options do you have? Plan small, realistic steps: don't try to do everything at once. Choose a few important goals: some things may have to go by the board. Praise yourself when you achieve a goal on the road to success.

"CHANGE the way you look at things and the things you look at will change." ~ Wayne Dyer, Author

5) TRY A DIFFERENT VIEW—STRESS experts agree that it is the way that we view events that creates stress. In 2013, research by *The European Heart Journal* found that those who *believed* stress affected their health 'a lot' or 'extremely' had a 50% greater risk of suffering a heart attack, even when researchers adjusted for biological, behavioral and psychological risk factors.   So if you want to reduce your stress levels you need to change the way you view stress and the things that cause you to feel stressed. It's the old glass half full or half empty battle! Here's a few helpful ways to do this:

A) REFRAME—CHANGE the way you see stressful things and situations, e.g., if a colleague at work is hassling or bullying you, instead of feeling threatened you could be grateful that you have an opportunity to learn and master assertiveness skills and to put these into practice; when you think you have problems, see them as challenges.

B) **Do a reality check**—LOOK at the here and now: will the things you are worrying about or stressing over ever happen? Where or what is your evidence? If it did happen, what would be the worst case scenario? Is that so bad? Will it kill you? Is there a way to minimize the risk of a bad outcome?

C) **Self-talk**—THOUGHT is energy, so it's critical to think and talk positive. Compelling research by Dr. Bruce Lipton, a developmental biologist best known for promoting the idea that genes and DNA can be manipulated by a person's beliefs, reveals that thoughts really do become things. If you want to create a positive outcome you must grow and foster positive beliefs – even if in the short-term you have to fake-it-to-make-it.

Resist saying things you don't want to make real. Instead of saying, "I can't cope," try replacing it with, "I can do this; I've handled change before," or, "I trust myself to be able to handle this.

To see confirmation of the power of language on your DNA view this clip on YouTube, where a water researcher from Japan, Dr. Emoto, demonstrates how thoughts really do change things. His water demonstration shows without doubt how your thoughts and intentions shape the physical world.

Positive messages create shiny, diamond-like reflective qualities while negative thoughts create deformed, collapsed structures with black holes and yellow tinged edges. We know this intuitively every time we're around someone who is negative but many stressed out people don't realize their negative, complaining, or angry energy is toxic to those around them. As Einstein once said, "everything is energy."

D) **Don't think in absolutes**—you'll only disappoint yourself.

Absolute statements like: "I *must* be perfect at everything I do *all the time*," or, "Everyone *must* like me, " or "I *always* have to be in control," is setting yourself up for failure.

These mistaken all-or-nothing beliefs are easily embraced during times of stress, but offer a false sense of security. It's OK, and very normal, not to be perfect.

It's also a myth that we're ever totally in control. Instead of saying, "I must," try a less absolute statement like, "I prefer things to be of a high standard." Or, "I like to be in control but I accept that this isn't always possible and that's ok too. I'm doing the best I can."

E) **RESIST FEELING LIKE A VICTIM**—LET go of negativity, no matter how justified you may feel. Don't focus on any bad aspects. For example, instead of complaining "Why me?" try saying, "It's a pain, but I'll deal with it." Or ask, "How can this problem or setback turn out for my highest good?"

I really like what Susan Jeffers, the author of Feel *The Fear and Do It Anyway*, encourages people to say during times of stress, "I constantly remind myself my life is unfolding in a perfect way. I trust the grand design."

6) **INCREASE YOUR COPING SKILLS**—IF you up-skill you'll minimize stress. Lots of people I have coached professionally have benefited from improving their: communication and assertiveness, ability to delegate, self-esteem, confidence and time management skills.

Others have benefited hugely from learning how to meditate. To download a free meditation tip sheet go to my website here >>

Other effective coping strategies may also include exercise or travel, taking breaks during the day, talking worries through, scheduling time off or taking time out. It never fails to amaze me how few people actually take lunch breaks! What three things could you do to increase your coping skills?

"WHEN YOU DWELL on all the reasons you have to be grateful, you open yourself to receiving even more good—and more good comes to you. As you begin to feel abundant, you'll be willing and able to pass positive things on to others." ~ *Oprah Winfrey, Talk Show Host*

7) ELIMINATE NEGATIVE EMOTIONS—AS you've already discovered everything, including your emotions, is energy. Negative emotions are toxic, robbing you of optimism and energy, and positive emotions create the opposite results.

One emotion that many clients who are unhappy at work experience is anger. Sometimes that anger is directed at themselves for not making changes earlier.

Anger can often kick in at times of frustration during job hunting activities too, when things don't go successfully.

When you trigger the stress response by getting angry it effectively disengages the cerebral cortex—the thinking part of the brain. That may be fine if you need to launch into defensive combat, but it doesn't help if you need to choose the best response and stop and muse on the merits of your chosen course of action.

Resist making huge life decisions when you're angry.

I KNEW of a man who made a dramatic change during a time of acute unhappiness. For over 15 years Martin had hated his job.

When he sold his shares in his business, an opportunity to reinvent his life appeared.

But lacking awareness of his transferrable skills and alternative career options he opted for self-employment in the same career. He assumed that the added flexibility and autonomy would give him back his mojo. Four years on he's disillusioned and angry.

"I'm a 53-year old fool. I hate what I do. I hate the person it makes me. I hate my clients: I think they're all pariahs."

In a fit of rage he decided to close down his business, take the hit, and put his house on the market.

'I'll get on a plane and leave. I can't afford to live here,' he said.

At the time I couldn't help but wonder how different the outcome may have been if he'd been proactive or sought professional help. What if he had spent more time thinking about what else he could do with his considerable skills and talents before he quit his business? What if he'd 'cut his cloth' earlier? I'm sure a more strategic, less dramatic change and reaction decision would have been reached. One with far better consequences.

In saying that, sometimes you have to know when it's time to quit, but planning, preparation and foresight go a long way. I guess you know that or you wouldn't be reading this book.

8) THINK AND GROW POSITIVE—TESTS of brain patterns show that positive thoughts trigger the production of feel-good hormones to areas of the brain responsible for positive emotions.

There is incredibly widespread ignorance of how emotions actually work. People struggle with the idea that we actually choose our emotions.

"He made me angry," one client said defensively. It's impossible for one human being to make another angry, sad, depressed or happy. There is always a point of choice. If you are struggling to

deal with negative emotions, seek advice from the experts—
remember a problem shared is a problem solved.

Be a guard for your words, thoughts and feelings, and call in the
cavalry. Think and grow positive—grab onto anything that makes
you feel better about yourself and what you have to offer. I believe
in a Higher Power, both within myself and in the unseen world—
holding onto my spirituality always comforts me during challenging
times.

9) TAP INTO YOUR PASSION—CHARLES Kovess, author of
Passionate People Produce, describes passion as: 'A source of
unlimited energy from the soul that enables people to achieve
extraordinary results.'

Often when you're feeling stressed, the things that you love to
do are the first things to be traded. When you tap into something
you deeply believe in and enjoy you may be amazed at the results.

Passion brings the energy or chi of love, giving you energy,
vitality and a heightened sense of well-being. It's one of the greatest
stress-busters of all, and promotes the generation of endorphins—
feel-good chemicals that will give you an extra spring in your step.
Even five minutes a day doing something you love can give you
your mojo back.

What may start off as a hobby could very well turn out to be a
fulfilling career. Like Brian Clifford, owner of Integrated Pest
Management, who had always been fascinated with bugs. After
becoming disenchanted with his first career, he opted to follow his
passion and became a 'pestie.' He loves the idea of being a white
knight coming to people's rescue.

What do you love doing? What inspires you? What makes you
feel joyful? Identify these things and make some time to go do it.
How could it lead you to a new career?

10) GET MOVING—DURING times of stress we can become lethargic. Feeling that we don't even have the energy or time to exercise may lead to feelings of depression as well as increased irritability.

Numerous studies have shown that exercise promotes the production of positive endorphins, which play a key role in making you feel better about yourself and your capacity to cope.

Research out of Princeton University now even suggests that regular physical activity may grow new brain cells. Exercise also helps to activate both hemispheres of your brain —bringing a new perspective as well as greater tolerance to life's stressors.

11) BREATHE—UNDER stress our breathing is reversed. Instead of breathing slowly and deeply our breathing tends to become shallower and more rapid. Under extreme stress we can forget to breathe at all. The actress Drew Barrymore had the words 'breathe' tattooed underneath her arm to remind her what to do during times of stress.

In a state of joy and relaxation, you breathe in a deep circular pattern, your heart comes into coherence and you begin to produce alpha brain waves, giving you access to your own natural tranquilizers and antidepressants.

Focusing on your breath and breathing deeply, can bring a state of calm and perspective during times of stress, allowing you to cope more effectively and to slow down or inhibit the stress response.

If you have forgotten how to breathe try this: breathe in deeply for a count of four, and exhale—slowing for a count of eight. Repeat 10 times. Notice how quickly your body and mind relaxes. Try this anywhere, anytime you notice feelings of stress returning and beat the stress response. Or tap into a meditation or yoga class for a mind-body makeover.

12) Tip the balance—it won't come as a surprise that lack of work-life balance increases stress. Research proves that people who organize their whole life around their work are more prone to high levels of stress and the development of post-traumatic embitterment disorder—a malady that covers almost every negative emotion a person can have at work.

Finding and prioritizing time for the things you enjoy is critical if you want to reduce your stress levels. Isolate all the key areas of your life and check to see if you have got the balance right.

13) KEEP A FOOD, and mood journal—this is one of the simplest biofeedback, self-help tools available.

"THE ONLY WAY TO keep your health is to eat what you don't want, drink what you don't like, and do what you'd rather not." ~ Mark Twain, Author

MANY STRESS COACHES encourage their clients to think of themselves as athletes. If you were a professional athlete, you would know whether you ran better in Nikes or Reeboks, whether your best times came after you ate steak and eggs for breakfast or granola.

Ask yourself, "What am I doing right?" Numerous studies suggest that people who keep journals manage to heal themselves on more than just psychological levels. Keeping track of your food and mood will help reinforce the behaviors that make you feel better, and be stronger about saying no to those which make you feel bad. You'll be more empowered and encouraged to tune into the higher intelligence of your body, mind and spirit.

14) FOOD FOR THE MIND, body and soul—reducing caffeine, alcohol, nicotine and other stimulants is a powerful way to feel better during times of stress. The trouble is that these sorts of stimulants are just the things people feel drawn to.

Like John who hates his job and tries to switch off by hitting the bottle, "I'm going to get a bottle of wine. It's the only way I can cope. I can't do this work without it."

Yet one drink leads to another and another, and before you know it cracks appear.

"I MADE a commitment to completely cut out drinking and anything that might hamper me from getting my mind and body together. And the floodgates of goodness have opened upon me, spiritually and financially." ~ Denzel Washington, Actor

Alcohol is a well documented neurotoxin—a toxic substance that inhibits, damages and destroys the tissues of your nervous system, especially your neurons, the conducting cells of your body's central nervous system.

If you can't knock out alcohol and other stimulants completely at least limit your intake. They all trigger the production of the stress-related hormone adrenaline, which increases the heart rate, prompts your liver to release more sugar into your bloodstream and makes your lungs suck in more oxygen.

While you may get a short-term energy spike or feeling of well-being, in the long run, you'll experience fatigue, low energy levels and even increased anxiety and depression—leading to a vicious cycle of relying on more stimulants to get you through the days and nights.

Are you worried about your drinking? Would you like to cut back or quit? Gain help and motivation, including sophisticated alcohol-free alternatives, in my book *Mind Your Drink: The Surprising Joy of Sobriety (Control Alcohol, Discover Freedom, Find Happiness and Change Your Life)*, available in print and eBook from all good bookstores.

Dying for a smoke? One of my clients started smoking during a period of stress. "I was bored," she said. "I just wanted to fit in with the people I was working with."

Aside from serious health implications you know about, like lung, brain and throat cancer, smoking robs the blood, muscles, brain and organs of oxygen, causing people to feel light-headed and tired and impeding optimal functioning.

Nicotine also increases levels of adrenaline and creates a vicious cycle of energy highs and lows. Cut down or stop. To help curb cravings, try taking a complex B vitamin supplement.

MIND FOOD

One of the best things you can also do to improve your stress resilience and well-being, and increase your chances of making a positive and sustainable change, is to improve your food and mental diet. There's a wealth of information on the web, but some of the things I've found really help are:

- Increasing my intake of fresh organic fruit and vegetables
- Reducing meat and dairy and processed foods
- Avoiding too much sugar and artificial energy boosts
- Cutting out booze

- Seeking professional help to identify allergies
- Meditation—The regular practice of meditation is scientifically proven to reduce stress and anxiety and to increase well-being. I love it!
- Essential oils—Another effective tool in your stress-busting kit is aromatherapy. Drop a few drops of one of the blends below onto a tissue and inhale for instant calm.

Blend #1: Three drops Clary Sage, one drop Lemon, one drop Lavender

Blend #2: Two drops Roman Chamomile, two drops Lavender, one drop Vetiver

Blend #3: Three drops Bergamot, one drop Geranium, one drop Frankincense

Blend #4: Three drops Grapefruit, one drop Jasmine, one drop Ylang Ylang

YOU'LL FIND MORE SCIENTIFICALLY ENGINEERED tips and holistic strategies to beat stress and boost happiness in my book *Stress Less. Love Life More: How to Stop Worrying, Reduce Anxiety, Eliminate Negative Thinking and Find Happiness.*

Action Question: Are You bored?

Did you know that being bored, under-challenged or not being able to do the things you care about are huge sources of stress? What's boring you about you current situation? How can you create some more challenge, learning or excitement, into your workday?

"Are you bored with life? Then throw yourself into some work

you believe in with all your heart, live for it. Die for it, and you will find happiness that you had thought could never be yours."
~ Dale Carnegie, Motivational Guru

What You've Learned So Far

- A degree of stress is a normal part of the career change and job search process. It gives you the energy you need to enjoy life and feel excitement and enthusiasm.
- Too much stress, however, can drown all the good feelings and create illness, depression, tension and self-doubt. Left unresolved too much stress can erode your will to live.
- Many people don't realize they're stressed and nearing burnout until it is too late. They soldier on or grit their teeth and bear whatever is causing the pain. They ignore early, medium and red alert warning signs that their body is giving them.
- Tune into your body barometer and listen for the physical, emotional, cognitive and behavioral signs of too much stress.
- Eliminate excess stress and build resilience by: identifying what's stressing you out; taking control; anticipating and preparing in advance; planning realistic solutions; trying a different view; reframing; doing a reality check; talking positively; resisting the urge to feel like a victim; increasing your coping skills; eliminating negative emotions; tapping into your passion; moving; breathing; regaining some balance; keeping a food, and mood journal; resting; and laughing.
- Remind yourself that stress is a normal part of life—it's

how you handle it that counts. Create a stress management plan and proactively manage your stress levels.

- Love it, don't leave it. Sometimes removing sources of stress in either your work or private life can mean falling back in love with your job.

What's next?

Now that we've looked at the factors driving and supporting your desire for change, and highlighted strategies to boost your spirit, let's look at more ways to to stay positive! The next chapter, will boost your resilience to setbacks and rediscover a sense of possibility for the future.

12

STAYING POSITIVE

EMBARKING on change of any sort requires courage, strength and resolve. Changing jobs is no exception. You may stumble upon some unanticipated obstacles in your path.

People who are important to you may actively discourage you and express doubt about your choices. Or you may face rejection along the way—missing out on roles you had applied for or not even making it to the interview stage.

This is normal.

The important thing is to stay positive and not give up. Take a leaf out of Thomas Edison's book. When asked why, after hundreds of unsuccessful attempts at inventing the light bulb, he didn't give up, he replied calmly "I have not failed, I have merely succeeded in finding ways that do not work".

Believe you can make it happen.

Now is the time to start developing the psychological "muscle" that will get you through the rough spots as you embark on your job search.

Dealing with Uncertainty

If you haven't set yourself some goals now is the time to do it. These will help provide the focus, the momentum, and the reason "why" to keep you moving forward.

However, while checklists and goal setting help, they can't eliminate all uncertainty and risk. Anxiety comes with uncertainty. The better prepared you are the less anxious you will be. Keep in mind that you are well prepared and maintain a positive outlook.

Affirmations: Positive Self- talk

One way to maintain a positive outlook is through affirmations. Affirmations are statements you can use to give yourself a boost when you experience doubt and uncertainty. When you feel discouraged, try repeating some of these statements as a way to steady yourself during the rough spots.

- "I always achieve my goals"
- "I always achieve whatever I conceive in my mind"

- "I'm gifted and energetic and I believe in myself"
- "I'm lucky to be here and the people I meet feel lucky to know me"
- "I am safe and all is well – everything is working toward my highest good"
- "My perfect role is coming to me now"
- "I deserve the best and people are happy to help me"

SAY these affirmations over and over again as many times a day as you need. You will be surprised at how the use of affirmative statements refocuses your energy in a positive way. The following exercise will help you develop your own affirmations.

Call To Action: Positive Self-talk

Everyone has had negative experiences that cause self-doubt. But our faith in our abilities to accomplish our goals can be re-enforced through affirmations. Repeating affirming statements is simply an acknowledgement of what you may already believe but may have come to doubt because of a bad experience.

Think about a situation that might make you feel uncomfortable, hesitant, or even fearful. Maybe it's making a phone call to a prospective employer to see if they have any vacancies or going for an interview. Whatever it might be, imagine yourself experiencing that same difficult situation in a way that you never have before—as your ideal self, confident, self-assured, at ease.

How do look in this fantasy? Describe yourself as you might look and feel:

Pick a few words that describe how you are in your fantasy.

Then develop an affirmation using those words to describe yourself in a positive, encouraging way.

Come up with more affirmations to encourage and support yourself.

Repeat the affirmations, eyes closed, putting your trust in the words you have chosen. How do you feel now?

REMEMBER: an affirmation is simply a statement acknowledging and affirming what it is that you already believe. Watch out for self-limiting beliefs that you may be affirming to your self such as: "I'll never get another job," "Nobody will want to hire me," or "I always get really nervous at interviews". These statements and others like them serve no other purpose than to prevent you from achieving your goals.

EXCERPT: MID-LIFE CAREER RESCUE (EMPLOY YOURSELF)

CHOOSE AND GROW YOUR OWN
BUSINESS WITH CONFIDENCE

Y ou don't always need buckets of money, or the courage of a
lion, to start your own business. Plenty of successful entrepreneurs have started their businesses on a shoe-string budget, and
launched new careers while combining salaried employment. Many
have felt the fear and launched their business anyway.

I was in my mid-30's, a single parent, holding down a steady
job, when I started my first business, Worklife Solutions. I was

worried and fearful that I'd fail, but I did it anyway. It's one of the most creative, joyful endeavors I've ever done. Since then I've created many more businesses and helped people all over the globe become successfully self-employed. Like some of people who share their story in this book, and other budding entrepreneurs who've taken a strategic route to finance their businesses.

When I first started out in business over a decade ago, I thought about all the people I knew, or had read about, that were successful in their own business. What I found then, still applies today. The list below is what they have in common. As you read this list think how many strategies could apply to you:

They were doing something they love; their passion drove them.

Making money was not their sole motivation. Their businesses grew from a desire to serve others; they were not trying to force something on others or to make a killer sale. Instead, they wanted to make a positive difference and create something of value. They didn't badger people into buying their goods or service.

1. **They cared about whether or not they could help a prospective client.** If they could, great. If not, they were either quietly persistent until they were needed, or they moved on.
2. **They planned for success.** Their business and marketing plans were living documents and they managed their finances extraordinarily well.
3. **They shared.** They communicated their vision, goals and plans with those important to them, and they researched their clients and stakeholders constantly to learn how to do things better *together*.
4. **They listened.** They listened to their staff, their families and their clients. Then, and only then, when they

understood their issues, fears, needs and desires did they offer a solution.

5. **They started smart.** When employing others, whether on contract or as salaried staff, they hired the right people for the right job, and employed people who were strong in areas they were not. When skills gaps appeared, they gave their people the training, systems, environment and recognition to do their job well.

6. **They took calculated risks.** They always looked before they leapt, but they leapt nonetheless. Courage and confidence was something they built as they went.

7. **They believed in themselves, or faked it!** Even professionals doubt themselves–but they don't let self-doubt win.

"YOU HAVE to believe in yourself. Even when you don't, you have to try," encourages Serena Williams, tennis super-star and 23-time Grand Slam champion.

"There are moments when I am on the court and I'm like, 'I don't think I'm going to be able to do this'. But then I fortify myself and say, 'I can, I can'–and it happens. If you believe in yourself, even if other people don't, that really permeates through and it shows. And people respect that."

IF THE STRATEGIES above sound like things you can do, or are willing to try, chances are self-employment is right for you. But to double check, try the following Entrepreneurial Personality Quiz.

THE ENTREPRENEURIAL PERSONALITY QUIZ

Do you have the right personality to be an entrepreneur? Are you better suited to becoming a Franchisee? Would contracting suit you better? Or is paid employment really the best option after all?

Before committing yourself to starting your own business of any type, you need to ask yourself whether you have what it takes.

The following quiz is written as though you are still in a salaried role. If you have already started your own business, respond to the questions as though you are still in your last job. Answer as you really are, not how you would like to be.

1. Is accomplishing something meaningful with your life important to you?
2. Do you typically set both short and long-term goals for yourself?
3. Do you usually achieve your goals?
4. Do you enjoy working on your own?
5. Do you like to perform a variety of tasks in your job?
6. Are you self-disciplined?

7. Do you like to be in control of your working environment?

8. Do you take full responsibility for your successes and failures?

9. Are you in excellent physical, mental, and emotional health?

10. Do you have the drive and energy to achieve your goals?

11. Do you have work experience in the type of business you wish to start?

12. Have you ever been so engrossed in your work that time passed unnoticed?

13. Do you consider 'failures' as opportunities to learn and grow?

14. Can you hold to your ideas and goals even when others disagree with you?

15. Are you willing to take moderate risks to achieve your goals?

16. Can you afford to lose the money you invest in your business?

17. When the need arises, are you willing to do a job that may not interest you?

18. Are you willing to work hard to acquire new skills?

19. Do you usually stick with a project until it is completed?

20. Does your family support and stand by you in everything you do?

21. Are you organized and methodical in your work?

22. Does it frustrate you when you can't buy the things you want?

23. Do you like taking calculated gambles?

24. Would you still want your own business, even if there were plenty of other good jobs?

25. Are you a people person?

26. Do you handle personal finances well?
27. As an employee did you/do you regularly suggest new ideas at various levels?
28. Do you feel that you can truly shape your own destiny?
29. How flexible are you when approaching work tasks? If things become difficult do you adapt and complete the task?
30. Is the money you could make one of the primary reasons for starting your own business?

Scoring:

Your answers to at least 20 of these questions should be yes if you are to be successful as a business owner.

The more 'yes' answers, the more likely you are to enjoy the entrepreneurial life and be successful as a business owner.

It is not necessary to answer yes to each of these questions, but if you answer no to some of them you will want to evaluate what that means to you and how significantly it may impact your ability to run your own business.

SUCCESS STORY: A FORK IN THE ROAD

Sheree Clark followed her enthusiasm—her passion for helping others and sharing what she had learned through her own life challenges led her to start her coaching business. The seeds of change were also cultivated during a stressful time in her life and her former job. She shares her journey of mid-life career reinvention below:

> "My current business is Fork in the Road. I am a healthy living (life) coach. I chose the name initially because I was focused on food and healthful eating, and since "fork" conjures up the idea of eating, it seemed to fit. I also believe that at any given point we are all at a proverbial fork in the road.
>
> That fork can be a major one—such as a career choice or the decision to enter or leave a marriage—or a small one, like whether to say yes to dessert or being on another committee. So, when the focus of my business shifted to life

coaching for women over 40, the name was still (and perhaps even more) fitting for my practice.

Fork in the Road is truly a crescendo of all of my life experience. I work with my clients to transform their health, reclaim vitality and mental focus, and help ensure they gain clarity on their vision and purpose. These are all things I have done for myself over the course of the last 6+ decades of life.

Deciding what to do

My first business was a marketing communications (advertising) agency that I was "talked into" co-founding in 1985 by a (then) new boyfriend. The truth is, I had grown bored at my job at a local university and had even announced my resignation, effective the following academic year (long notices are an accepted practice at US academic institutions). In the meantime, I had met—and fallen in love with—my later-to-be business partner, and the rest fell into place.

He convinced me that my skill set as a teacher, advisor and mentor would transfer easily to the business development aspect of running an advertising agency. We stayed business partners for 25 years (although the romantic aspect tanked after the initial 14 years).

My current business began after I decided to leave the agency world and (my now-ex) behind.During my time owning the agency, I had taken a variety of classes simply out of an interest in personal development. Many of the courses had to do with health, nutrition and emotional maturity.

Eventually, as I became less interested in the marketing work and more involved in the business of human potential, it became harder to rally enthusiasm for owning an agency. Finally, just as we were preparing to commemorate 25 years in business together, I told my partner I wanted to exit our partnership to begin something new. At that point, I still wasn't certain what my new work would look like, but I knew it wasn't fair to anyone (most especially me!) to stay where I knew I was no longer fully engaged.

So, in essence, I quit—and then I figured it out.

Finding an idea that would be successful—ask your way to success

I found the right product for the right market by trial and error! Next to creating a vision board, the informational interview is my favorite tool for helping me get back on track when I'm feeling lost.

When I was feeling unfulfilled in my business I scheduled a series of interviews with fellow entrepreneurs. I picked women who owned businesses. The only thing they had in common was that I really respected them, even though some I had never met in person.

One of my interviews was with the publisher of a local business newspaper: a fabulous lady who is probably 20 years my senior. We had our meeting over lunch and I told her, candidly, about my inner feelings. I told her I was hoping she might shed some light.

I asked her what she thought my skill sets and offerings were and where I might be able to plug the gaps. Her feedback? She said she had always thought of me as a teacher and a coach. She said she saw me as articulate, smart and capable, (which in itself is nice to hear, especially coming from someone you admire).

And then she offered up a casual suggestion. She said,

"You've always had a way with words. Why don't you write a column for a publication in your industry or some area of your life that brings you joy." Well, that was an idea that resonated, and if nothing else was worth seeing if I could make happen.

The payoff

I went back to my office and sent a query letter to the editor of a graphic design magazine I had written for once or twice before, and asked if they were looking for writers.

Within an hour my phone rang. It was the editor himself. His words nearly knocked me off my chair. He said, "Wow, what timing! We are starting a business advice column in the next quarter, wanna write it?"

I ended up writing that column for five years. Not only did it help scratch an itch I was feeling, I made some extra money in the process. Now, I am not saying you'll have such epic results. But I do know that I have never had an informational interview without a payoff, even if it was just that I got to know somebody a little better.

Working your offerings into your own area of genius

It's not just about finding the right products and services, it's also about working your offerings into your own area of genius.

At this point in my life, while I enjoy making a good income, it's not only about maximizing revenue. I want to do work that brings me joy. I want to work with clients who are a fit for me, so that when I look at my calendar/schedule, I feel excitement, rather than dread.

In my instance, I am what we call a "Baby Boomer" (defined in the USA as being those born between 1946 and

1965). My generation and those slightly after, are all experiencing some major life challenges right now. Our jobs are changing or we've been laid off or deemed "redundant."

Our marriages and family structures are shifting or crumbling: we may suddenly become caretakers or divorcees or widows. Hell, our own bodies are changing and often it feels as though they are betraying us. And for many women over 40, after putting the needs of others first for much of our lives, we can finally say, "it's MY turn now."

What I just described is my area of genius. It's the arena I do best in and it's where I feel most at home. Having for the most part successfully navigated the challenges of being a 40, 50, 60-year old, I get to share my secrets and techniques with other women.

Starting fresh—financing a new career

In both cases when I started my companies I left what I had been doing to embark on the new thing. In the first instance (co-founding the agency) I felt safe doing so because I had a partner and so my risk/exposure was shared.

In the second instance (becoming a coach), I had the luxury of having built savings from the first endeavour, so I could plunge into the second. I recognize that not everyone will have such good fortune.

In both cases, I didn't need any start-up capital.

If I were to give advice, I'd say that while of course you have to consider your own financial situation, also take stock of your risk tolerance.

Entrepreneurship is not certain. There are all sorts of risks and no guarantees. If a lack of financial uncertainty makes you nervous, it's certainly safer to ease into being a business owner, but it can also be more challenging. There are only so many hours in a day!

Finding the confidence to leave the security of a regular salary

It wasn't confidence that propelled me into my second business. It was the pain of not living authentically.

It would be an understatement to say that to close the ad agency I had co-founded was not a decision my former partner and I made easily or lightly. For almost half our lives we had been partners and close friends. But the time had come and we each wanted to do other things with our lives.

I had found a passion in the health and nutrition arena after receiving my certifications as a raw vegan chef and nutrition counselor. My business partner discovered a love of fine art and a desire to work more independently. Quite frankly, we both had become rather miserable in our roles as principals and we each needed new challenges.

Despite my excitement for my new future I struggled to dismantle what we had so carefully created. At the time, we decided to close the agency, it was still healthy but my partner's and my passions were on life support.

There were many signs that it was time for a change. I started to dread the out of town travel for clients that I had once so loved. He began to come into the office later and leave earlier.

We both had less patience for employee mistakes and client indecision. For me the defining moment came on a Sunday at church when I actually cried not because the sermon was so moving, but because I knew that in less than 24 hours I had to "go back to work."

It was clearly time to do something.

There are those who have applauded both of us for having the courage to do something so drastic, and others who deem us insane when we could be 'so close to retirement.' All I know is that, as scary as it was, it has rekindled the adrenalin rushes I have not felt in a very, very long time. It was absolutely the right thing to do.

Finding customers

My clients typically follow me online for a period of time before contracting with me for services. Often they run across me because I am a guest speaker at live events, or a subject matter expert on television, or a guest on an online interview series or summit. Others may have been referred to me by a friend or a colleague.

The marketing activities which have been most important and successful for me are speaking and interviews. I also write guest blogs and articles.

Maintaining balance

Running a business should not be a 24/7 thing! Although there are absolutely "push" times, especially in the beginning, I think down time and rest are essential to business success

Down time, time to refuel, is made possible by setting priorities, delegation and hiring (or subcontracting) efficiently. I personally find balance by planning my days the night before. Each night before I go to bed, I establish what the most important project or priority is for the next day, and that project is the first thing I address after I do my exercise and meditation.

I also find that sometimes I have to actually schedule in my fun times. With my current work schedule, I coach clients the first three weeks of the month. The last week of every month I take off from individual coaching, and that is when I attend to personal matters such as doing errands, scheduling salon services and meeting friends for social engagements. I still do work during that fourth week, but because I don't typically schedule client appointments, I have time for other things.

Keeping energy levels high

It's not hard to have high energy when you have high enthusiasm. I love what I do and it keeps me young, vital, engaged and energized. That said, taking care of yourself mentally emotionally and spiritually is also critical. I get adequate sleep, exercise and nutrition. I spend time in nature and in contemplation or prayer.

I have deep relationships. AND I have a coach. That may sound odd, because I AM a coach, but I believe those of us who are most successful, have gotten where we're at with help in identifying blocks, challenges and opportunities. That is what a coach does!

The secret to success, managing cash flow, and generating regular income

For me personally, I have always benefitted from finding and utilizing a good business coach and what is often called a 'mastermind community.' A mastermind is a group of like-minded people who meet regularly to share strategies and tackle challenges and problems together. They lean on each other, give advice, share connections and do business with each other when appropriate.

It's very much peer-to-peer mentoring, and it works! In terms of managing cash flow: one piece of advice is to not take your foot off the 'new business development' gas pedal when you get busy with other things. What you do today will determine your level of success tomorrow.

The learning curve

The biggest learning curve I had was going from owning a company that sold its services in a business to business arena (the communications agency) to one that provided services via a business to consumer model (my coaching practice).

These two ways of conducting business are drastically different. Again, by seeking guidance from peers and by hiring a coach I was able to manage the amount of growing pain.

The best times in my business have usually been the "firsts." First client, first employee, first million-dollar year. The worst have usually been the result of going against my own intuition. Hiring someone I had a gut feeling about because they looked good on paper. Taking a poorly calculated risk because I was listening to my ego instead of looking at the facts or my intuition.

One of the best business books I have read is, *Turning Pro* by Steven Pressfield. It applies to everyone, but entrepreneurs especially.

What advice would you give to someone who has never started a business or been self-employed?

Start by taking the time to meet with other entrepreneurs and ask them a few questions about things that may have you concerned or sparked your curiosity. This book, *Mid-Life Career Rescue: Employ Yourself,* is a great start, because it gives you a general 'peek under the tent' at being a business owner, but I would also speak to others in real time. I often urge my clients to schedule what I refer as an 'informational interview' when they are considering going down new paths or are feeling stuck in some area of their lives.

What are the steps to self-employment? Is there a "right" order?

I have taken the leap to self-employment twice, and each time was different from the other. I think there are too many factors to make a generalized bit of advice valuable here. One caveat I would say to the analytical readers is "don't overthink it."

With my current business, I began by sending a letter to everyone I knew from my former business, telling them what I was transitioning to, and straight-out asking them if they might be interested in my services, or if they would be willing to make a referral. I had enough takers to be encouraged to keep going!

Making the leap sooner

I would have left my first company to start my second company sooner. I was afraid of letting people down: my former partner, my employees, my clients. By the time I left, my passion was on life support.

If I could offer one piece of advice related to starting your own business and employing yourself it would be to know that being an entrepreneur can be lonely sometimes. Your friends, the ones who are employed by others, will think you have it made now.

They will believe that you have all the time in the world to do what you want, and that you're rolling in the money.

They'll think you can go on lavish vacations and that you don't have to answer to anyone. Take heart: The other business owners you meet will know the real story.

The secret to self-employed success

Passion. Without it you may be mildly successful, but you'll never be wildly successful!"

Find out more about Sheree's passion-driven business here—www.-fork-road.com. Listen to our interviews here http://www.cassandra-gaisford.com/media and http://www.cassandragaisford.com/podcast/

I loved, loved, loved what Sheree shared and devoured every word —best of all there were no calories…so that was marvellous. What resonated with you?

Identify and record any lessons can you learn from Sheree's experience of discovering her calling and setting up her business which you could apply to starting your own business. Summarize some possible action steps.

WHAT YOU'VE LEARNED SO FAR

- Before committing yourself to starting your own business or being self-employed, you need to ask yourself whether you have what it takes
- Follow your heart, let your passion and intuition guide you towards the business you were born to create
- You have to believe in yourself—even when you don't
- You don't always need buckets of money, or the courage

of a lion, to start your own business. You can start on a shoe-string and feel the fear and begin anyway

- Starting a business doesn't have to be a full-time gig. You can start small and keep your current job while you watch your baby grow
- Caring about people and delivering something of value is the key to success

What's Next?

So, now you know the pitfalls of being self-employed and you know some of the joys. But do you really understand what YOU are looking for and why?

The next chapter will help you clarify the motivating forces driving your decisions. Knowing these will help boost your confidence when it comes to making an inspired leap.

WHY DO YOU WANT TO BE YOUR OWN BOSS?

"Wild horses wouldn't drag me back
to working for someone else."
Alan Sugar, Entrepreneur and host of The Apprentice, UK

So now you know the pitfalls of being self-employed and you

know some of the joys. But do you really understand what YOU are looking for and why?

Perhaps you can identify with Laura who wants to balance work commitments with caring for her young son. "My boss insists I go to the office. I can't understand why he won't let me work from home."

Do Your Own Thing

Creating your own business is one of the few ways you can generate an income doing what you want, when you want, with whom you want.

It can also be a great way to create an asset—one you can grow and sell later for a profit if you plan things right.

Employing yourself is also a great way to get a job when nobody else will hire you, or when you've lost your job. Like Wendy Pye (her story is shared below), who started her own company and went from redundant to becoming a multi-millionaire.

Running your own business doesn't mean that you are going to be chained to your desk 24/ 7 as some people mistakenly believe. One of the important things prior to starting any new venture is to determine what you want to achieve and why.

Action Task! Clarify what you really want

Write a list of benefits that self-employment will offer you. If you run out of ideas the following list may help. Identify how you want to feel, and what you want to have, and why this is important to you.

Benefits of Self Employment

Listed below are some of the benefits many people gain from being self-employed. Make a note of those most relevant to you and add these to the list you generated above.

Assess any options you are considering by creating a decision-making criteria checklist. For example, if time freedom is important for you, you may want to reconsider any plans to open a business where people expect you to be there at fixed hours.

- Time freedom—hours to suit yourself
- Flexibility
- No forced retirement age
- Autonomy
- Independence
- Making your own decisions
- Creativity
- Control
- Security–not worrying about corporate layoffs
- Live and work anywhere in the world
- Work from home
- Accountability
- Higher earnings
- Satisfaction and personal fulfillment
- Variety and freedom to be able to work on new ideas and create your own authentic style
- Combine diverse areas of interest, skill and enthusiasm
- Being guided by what feels right in your heart and intuition
- Freedom from financial stress
- Making a difference
- Freedom from the daily grind—a business that runs without you
- Being able to put all your passion and energy into

something you believe in, rather than something
someone else believes in

- Creating an income producing asset

From Redundant to Multi-Millionaire

Necessity, as some say, is the mother of invention–and often it is the extra push many people need to take a leap into something new.

Some 55,000 New Zealanders are so-called 'necessity entrepreneurs,' people prompted by redundancy or unemployment to set up their own businesses, as distinct from 'opportunity entrepreneurs,' who've become self-employed as a result of planning and choice.

Wendy Pye is the mother of all necessity entrepreneurs. It took a good dose of adversity to get her entrepreneurial juices flowing and she hasn't looked back. She was dumped without warning from NZ News after 22 years with the company, given five minutes to clear her desk, and then marched off the premises.

With no job to go to Pye, then aged 42, set up her own educational publishing company. Now a multi-millionaire, she admits her motivation for going it alone was a desire to show her former employers what she could do.

"I was devastated and disappointed. But it really changed my life, which is a lot better now than if [redundancy] had never happened. I needed the push."

She certainly showed her former employers just what she could do. The 2015 National Business Review's Rich List, estimates Pye's personal wealth at $105 million.

She has fond thoughts for that executive who laid her off all those years ago. "That guy had vision," she says. "He knew something I didn't know. I can say that and laugh now."

Dubbed one of New Zealand's women powerbrokers, Dame

Wendy recently won the Business Entrepreneur category in the Women of Influence Awards.

The passion, determination and drive that helped her build her business into one of the most successful education export companies in the world shows no sign of slowing as she heads into her 70s.

Wendy Pye Publishing can now celebrate more than 2000 titles, in more than 20 countries, which have sold over 218 million copies. Her business has also developed digital learning platforms designed to teach children to read and write.

AGE IS **On Your Side**

Age is no barrier to employing yourself. Growing numbers of 40-plus men and women are taking up new challenges and starting businesses everyday. Being your own boss gives you more control over your future. If you love what you're doing, chances are you'll never want to retire.

Your life expectancy is on the rise. Which also means you'll be wanting enough money to live comfortably. Employing yourself will help you achieve that.

READY TO LEARN **some new tricks?**

As Brian Jones writes in his wonderful book, *Over 50? Start Your Business: Build Wealth, Control Your Destiny. Leave a Legacy*: "Within the last twenty years, technologies such as functional magnetic response imaging (FMRI) have debunked the old-dog-new-tricks myth. Scientists have found that the brain can grow and make new connections at any age. The scientific term for this is neuroplasticity.

Now more than ever you can be, do and have nearly anything

you desire. Like Annie, who aged 54, left teaching and became a
romance writer.

COMPELLING EVIDENCE of Mid-Life Success

Loads of people have employed themselves or started their businesses in mid-life and beyond. Here's just a few:

- Joseph Campbell started Campbell's soup at age 52
- Arianna Huffington started the Huffington post at age 54
- Estee Lauder founded her cosmetics empire when she was 54
- Charles Flint started IBM at 61
- Amadeo Giannini founded the Bank of America when he was 60
- Col. Harlan Sanders launched KFC at age 65
- Heather Morris was 64 when she became a full-time author following her debut success with the publication of *The Tattooist of Auschwitz*

WILL YOU BE NEXT? What are you waiting for? If they can do it there's a strong likelihood you can too.

ACTION TASK! Look For Your Heroes

Gather examples of mid-life entrepreneurs who inspire you. Allow them to be your virtual mentors. How can you use their success to guide and encourage you?

WHAT YOU'VE LEARNED SO FAR

- Intensify your desire, but keep it real. Get clear about what you want to gain by being your own boss and why
- Assess any options you are considering by creating a decision-making criteria checklist
- Sometimes life 'shouts' and gives you the push you need to start your business
- Courageous action can be inspired even at what seems

the worst of times. If life is dealing you a raw hand look
for opportunities that may be disguised as setbacks
- Age is no barrier to self-employment

What's Next?

Now you have a clearer idea about both your 'what' and your
'why' is, and you have awakened your desire. The next step is to
work out exactly what sort of business or self-employment opportunity is right for you.

To do this there is no better place to start than to determine what
sets your heart on fire.

PURSUE YOUR PASSION NOT YOUR PENSION

"The starting point of all achievement is desire."
Napoleon Hill, Author

FIRST THINGS FIRST! Start from the heart.

The first and most important commandment of choosing and growing your business is to follow your passion.

Creating a successful business that you'll love is impossible without passion, enthusiasm, zest, inspiration and the deep satisfaction that comes from doing something that delivers you some kind of buzz.

Passion is a source of energy from the soul, and when you combine it with a product or service that benefits others, that's where you'll find your magic.

Kevin Roberts, former CEO worldwide of advertising agency Saatchi and Saatchi, passionately believes that love is the way forward for business. Meeting peoples' needs, hopes, dreams, and desires, or offering something which helps them solve problems for which they'd love a cure, is good for people and its good for business.

"For great brands to survive, they must create Loyalty Beyond Reason," he writes in his book *Lovemarks: The Future Beyond Brands*. Roberts argues, with a ton of facts, and emotionally evocative images to support his premise, that traditional branding practices have become stultified. What's needed are customer Love affairs. "The secret," he maintains, "is the use of Mystery, Sensuality, and Intimacy."

Other experts such as Simon Sinek, author of the bestselling book *Start With Why*, and Robert Kiyosaki entrepreneur and author of the *Rich Dad, Poor Dad* books, may urge you to begin with rational, head-based logic.

I'm advocating a similar, albeit less analytical approach to begin with. But the premise is similar, to create something meaningful for yourself, and for the customers and clients you wish to attract, you must believe in what you are doing. Your business idea must matter. You must know *why* it's important—to yourself and to others.

"'*Why*' is not money or profit—these are always the results. Why does your organization exist? Why does it do the things it does? Why do customers really buy from one company or another?" challenges Sinek in his book.

I would add, *what* is its purpose? Roberts, would add, *how* can you make them fall in love with you and inspire loyalty beyond reason?

How to Find Your *Why*

When you discover and tap into your passion, you'll find your *why*. You'll also find a huge source of untapped potential that seems to be fearless and knows no bounds. Pursuing your passion in business is profitable on many levels.

Firstly, when you do what you love, this is most likely where your true talent lies, so you'll stand out in your field. Passion cannot be faked.

Secondly, you will be more enthusiastic about your pursuits. You will have more energy and tenacity to overcome obstacles, and more drive and determination to make things happen.

When you do what you care most about and believe in with such a passion, your work will be not something that you endure, but something that you enjoy. More importantly, work will become a vehicle for self-expression.

Thirdly, passion attracts. As multi-millionaire businesswoman Anita Roddick once said, '*We communicate with passion and passion sells.*'

Ms Roddick founded her company, The Body Shop, on one simple premise—beauty products tested on animals was cruel, barbaric, unnecessary and immoral. Millions of men and women around the world agreed.

People like to do business with people who are passionate about their products and services. When global financial services company KPMG re-branded with passion as a core theme, profitability soared. Check out my presentation on Slideshare to find out how:

http://www.slideshare.net/CassandraGaisford/passionslides-with-kpmg-slides

HEARTS ON FIRE

The key to sound business planning begins from the inside out. First you need to determine who you are, who you want to be, and what you want to contribute to the world. In working this out, there is no better place to start than with finding out what sets you heart on fire and *why*.

Michael Jr. Comedy, a stand-up comedian and author, explains how discovering your *why* helps you develop options that enable you to live and work with purpose.

"When you know your *why*, you have options on what your *what* can be. For instance, my *why* is to inspire people to walk in purpose. My *what* is stand-up comedy. My *what* is writing books.... Another *what* that has moved me toward my *why* is a web series that we have out now called Break Time."

Check out this clip from one of Michael's most successful episodes http://bit.ly/1PnOTrH. You'll see how working with passion and purpose awakens dormant talents and enables souls to fly higher.

"When you know your *why* your *what* has more impact because you are walking toward your purpose," says Michael.

WE'LL DIVE DEEPER into discovering your life purpose in the following chapter.

SURF THE WEB

http://www.eofire.com: Fuel your inspiration by checking out this top-ranked business Podcast where some of the most inspiring entrepreneurs are interviewed 7-days a week. Founder and host John Lee Dumas shares his journey from frustrated employee to inspired entrepreneur via video here http://www.eofire.com/about/

DISCOVERING Your Passion

Everyone is capable of passion; some people just need help taking it out of the drawer. Look for the clues. Often this involves noticing the times you feel most energized and alive, or when you experience a surge of adrenaline through your body.

Sometimes it's the moments when time seems to fly. Perhaps it is something you love to do and would willingly do for free.

Passion is not always about love. The things that push your buttons can lead you to the things that you're most passionate about.

Working long hours, too much stress, financial strain or a whole raft of other constant pressures can soon send you drowning in a sea of negativity—killing your passion and robbing you of the energy and positivity you need to make a life-enhancing change.

If stress is taking a toll on your life you may want to check out the first book in the *Mid-Life Career Rescue* series, *The Call For Change*. The strategies and tips in the book will help you restore the balance and get your mojo back. You'll also learn how to boost your ability to generate ideas to get unstuck. Available on Amazon in paperback and eBook by clicking the following link >> getBook.at/CareerChange

If you need more help to you manage stress my book, *Stress Less. Love Life More: How to Stop Worrying, Reduce Anxiety, Eliminate Negative Thinking and Find Happiness*, available as a paperback and Ebook will help. Navigate to here —getBook.at/StressLess.

ACTION TASK! Find Your Passion

Real passion is more than a fad or a fleeting enthusiasm. It can't be turned on and off like a light switch. Answering the following questions will help you begin to clarify the things you are most passionate about:

1. **When does time seem to fly?** When was the last time you felt really excited, or deeply absorbed in, or obsessed by something? What were you doing? Who were you with? What clues did you notice?

2. **What do you care deeply or strongly about?** Discovering all the things that you believe in is not always easy. Look for the clues to your deep beliefs by catching the times you use words such as 'should' or 'must.'

3. **What do you value?** What do you need to experience, feel, or be doing to feel deeply fulfilled?

4. **What pushes your buttons or makes you angry?** How could you use your anger constructively to bring about change?

5. **Which skills and talents come most easily or naturally to you?** Which skills do you love using? What skills do you look forward to using? What gives you such a buzz or a huge sense of personal satisfaction that you'd keep doing it even if you weren't paid?

6. **What inspires you?** To be inspired is to be in spirit. What bewitches and enthralls you so much that you lose all track of time? What makes your soul sing? What floats your boat? What things, situations, people, events etc. fill you with feelings of inspiration? List all your obsessions and the things that interest you deeply. If you're struggling to identify your interests and inspirations, you'll find some handy prompts in the next chapter.

7. **Keep a passion journal.** My passion is passion—to help others live and work with passion and to bring about positive change in the world. If you're not sure what you are passionate about, creating a passion journal is one simple but powerful technique to help achieve clarity. Your passion journal is where manifesting your preferred future really happens. I've been keeping a passion journal for years and so many things I've visualized and affirmed on the pages, are now my living realities— personally and professionally.

Love Is Where The Magic Is

Love is where the magic is. When you love what you do with such a passion you'd do it for free this is your path with heart. You've heard the saying, 'when you do what you love, you'll never work again.' It's true. Work doesn't feel like a slog, it feels energizing.

As Annie Featherston, writing as Sophia James, shared in the second book on the *Mid-Life Career Rescue* series, *What Makes You Happy*, "When you combine your favorite skills with doing something you completely and utterly love, you come home to your True

Self and find your place of bliss. The result? Contentment—and more often than not, producing something highly marketable."

PASSION IN BUSINESS

A good way to find your own passion and identify ways to turn it into a fulfilling self-employment opportunity is to look for examples of others who have started businesses they are passionate about.

Here are just a few of many examples:

A PASSION FOR BUGS! Brian Clifford is passionate about helping people and bugs. He has combined his passion into a successful business as a pest controller.

"All the rats, all the maggots, all the cockroaches all over the place, these are the things that I love doing,' he says. His business motto is, 'If it bugs you, I'll kill it!'"

Check out his business here >> www.borercontrolwellington.co.nz

A PASSION FOR BONES! John Holley has turned his passion for bones into a business, Skulls Down Under, selling skeletons to museums all over the world.

Check out his business here >> www.skullsdownunder.co.nz

A PASSION FOR MAORI FOOD. Charles Royal's passion for finding a way to incorporate traditional Maori foods into modern dishes led him to start his own business—Kinaki Wild Herbs.

"I had learned a lot about the bush during my time in the army and have taken that knowledge through the years, developing food tours and cooking classes using what we gather from the wild. I love organics and making something out of nothing, but you have to know what you are looking for," says Royal. Air New Zealand now serves pikopiko and horopito in its First and Business Classes.

Check out his business here >> www.maorifood.com

SUCCESS STORY: A LOVE OF GOOD FOOD

"**P**assion is Everything—If You Don't Have It You Will Not Succeed"

A love of good food and a lifelong dream to open their passion-driven business in London fueled Wellington restauranteurs Vivienne Haymans and Ashley Sumners' move to the UK.

"We both felt we had gone as far as we could with our business in New Zealand and wanted to move further afield," says Vivienne.

"I came here for a three-month holiday, secretly wanting to stay longer and build a business overseas. On arriving I discovered that London seriously needed a restaurant like our Sugar Club in Wellington. There was nowhere in London doing anything like it. I called Ash and a year later he also moved to London after selling our Wellington restaurant."

They relocated the restaurant to Notting Hill in 1995, then to Soho in 1998, winning the Time Out "Best Modern British Restaurant" award in 1996 and "Best Central London Restaurant" award in 1999, along with several Evening Standard Eros awards.

Since then they have expanded and diversified their restaurant business, opening a chain of modern *traiteurs* (Italian-style delicatessens) that offer delicious, easy-to-prepare hand-made meals and great New Zealand coffee.

The first of these is called The Grocer on Elgin, situated in the heart of Notting Hill. Vivienne designed all three restaurants and 'The Grocer on' stores.

Like many people following their passion, Vivienne and Ash faced significant barriers before finally making it big.

"It took Ash and I seven years to fulfill our dream of opening The Sugar Club in London. When we first arrived there were huge premiums being asked for restaurant sites.

Then, with the early 90s recession they were giving restaurants away but, like now, the banks were not lending. We had no property assets at the time, limited funds, a reference from our NZ lawyer, accountant and bank manager and a handful of NZ press clippings. The banks wanted property assets and UK business records. No less."

Just when it looked like the obstacles were insurmountable, their passion for great food and design, the quality of the produce, and the integrity of its production, produced lucky fruit.

"We were offered a site by a landlord that we had had dealings with in the past. He liked what we did and gave us the lease. We developed the old Singapore Pandang into the Notting Hill Sugar Club. I borrowed an extra £5000 from my mum and paid her back in a month. It was an instant success and well worth the long wait."

Vivienne says that following their passion is an important ingredient in their success.

"Passion is everything—if you don't have it you will not succeed. It is hard work; your passion will pull you through the seriously bad times, which will always occur."

Hot Tip! Gathering your own examples of passionate people and businesses is a great way to build confidence and generate your own business ideas.

Here are some things that other people who are self-employed are passionate about:

- **Creating Businesses**—Entrepreneurs Melissa Clarke Reynolds and Eric Watson
- **Airports**—Graham is an airport designer
- **Boats**—Bill Day runs a specialist maritime service business
- **Beauty**—Joy Gaisford, Designer
- **Food**—Ruth Pretty, Caterer and food writer
- **Astronomy**—Richard Hall, Stonehenge Aotearoa
- **Design**—Luke Pierson, runs a web design business
- **Rocks**—Carl created Carlucciland—a rock-themed amusement park
- **Passion**—Cassandra Gaisford helping people work and live their passion!

Here are some things that some businesses are passionate about:

- **Animal Welfare and Human Rights**—The Body Shop
- **Technology**—Microsoft, Apple
- **Helping people**—Worklife Solutions, Venus Network

- **Equality**—The EEO Trust, and the Johnstone Group
- **The Environment**—The Conservation Department
- **Honey**—The Honey Hive
- **Chocolate**—Chocaholic
- **Pampering Others**—East Day Spa

TUNE In To Your Body Barometer

What pushes your buttons or makes you angry? Having my manager threaten to 'smash my head in,' and working with others who were bullies and tyrants, the relentless pursuit of profit at the expense of caring for people, and numerous work restructurings, motivated me to gain my independence.

That and getting shingles—something I wrote about in my first books, *The Call for Change*, and also *What Makes You Happy.*

Shingles was definitely my body barometer sending me a red alert! As was seeing my colleagues suffer heart attacks.

As Neale Walsch, the author of *Conversations with God,* says, "Judge not about which you feel passionate. Simply notice it, then see if it serves you, given who and what you wish to be."

So, as I've mentioned earlier, rather than become bitter, I thought how could I use my anger constructively to bring about change?

I decided I wanted to help people find jobs that made them happy, and I wanted to help victims of workplace bullying. That was my *why* and my *what*.

STEPPING Stones to Success

I started a career counseling business for an established workplace counseling organization before going out on my own.

Working as an employee first gave me the confidence to fly free. I became more motivated when the CEO changed and the new boss tried to manage me. Increasingly, the job began to frustrate me.

It lacked challenge, my salary was capped, and I was finding it increasingly difficult to balance childcare. The final clincher however was when I did the math.

I worked out my hourly rate as a full-time salaried employee, versus what they charged me out per hour, and how much business I was bringing in for them, and came to the conclusion they were buying my skills, but they weren't paying me enough. I could work less and earn and achieve more if I employed myself. I started to feel excited!

ACTION TASK! Tune into Your Body Barometer

Notice the times you feel strong emotions. These could be annoyance, irritation and anger. Or they could be a sense of excitement, a state of arousal, a feeling of limitless energy, a burning desire, a strong gut feeling, a feeling of contentment or determination. Notice these feelings and record them in your passion journal.

Go deeper. Ask, "How could I make a living from my passion?" or "How do others make a living from things that excite or motivate me?"

Explore possibilities. Even a simple Google search, or generating ideas with others could get you started down the right path.

** FREE BONUS **

If you haven't downloaded the free copy of the Passion Workbook, download it here
>>http://worklifesolutions.leadpages.co/free-find-your-passion-workbook.

WHAT YOU'VE LEARNED SO FAR

- Passion is energy. It is emotion, zest, intensity, enthusiasm and excitement. Passion is love
- Creating more love in the world is the way forward for business. Meeting peoples' needs, hopes, dreams and desires, or offering something which helps them solve problems for which they'd love a cure, is good for people and its good for business

- Do what moves you. Pursuing your passion, not your pension, can be a liberating and clarifying catalyst to your true calling and the business you were born to create

- A healthy obsession can lead to many things. Not only will your passion lead you to your path with heart, it will also help fuel the fires of determination, courage and self-belief. You'll be fully alive, stand out from the crowd and gain a competitive edge

- If you don't know where to look, passion can be difficult to find. Tune into your body barometer and notice the times when you feel most alive, inspired or fulfilled

- Start a passion journal—keep track of the times when you notice clues to your passion, such as a feeling of inspiration or any of the other signs discussed in this chapter. Record these moments so that they don't get lost or forgotten

- Adding quotes, pictures or any other insights will really make your journal come alive. Gain greater awareness of what drives your passion by asking yourself, "Why am I passionate about this?" Look for the themes and patterns that build up over time

- Keep your passion alive by updating your journal and referring to it regularly. Actively look for examples of people who have made the things you are passionate about into a rewarding business

What's Next?

In the next chapter you'll discover how joyous and exciting work and life is when you're working with a higher purpose.

Did you enjoy this excerpt?

Grab The Ultimate Guide to Freedom

Mid-Life Career Rescue: Employ Yourself

Start a business on the side while holding down your job. Or take the leap to self-employed bliss. Choose and grow your own business with confidence. This handy resource will show you how.

Available in print and eBook.

AFTERWORD

Writing *my Mid-Life Career Rescue series* has given me the confidence, the security, the faith, the power of belief, and the validation that following your passion is the only way to live.

I write what I believe. I write what I feel. I write what I want to read. And I write to help myself.

If my words inspire you, if my words make a difference, if my words empower you to make a change for the better, then I am happy. Thrilled. Elated. But it will not have been because of me—it will have been because of you.

You are the one who has changed. I will have had the privilege of providing a spark, a light, a beam to shine along your sacred path. But you will have taken the route less travelled. If not now, soon :)

Thank you for trusting me to guide you. I really hope you loved this book as much as I loved writing it. And I hope it aids your growth, as I have grown and flourished as I wrote.

Mostly, I hope this book in particularly has helped you confidently leave a job you hate, find a job you adore, and start living a life you love.

Please keep in touch. Write to me, if you feel like it, and let me know how you're doing. I promise to write back.

I invite you to share your stories and experiences in our Career Rescue Community. We'd love to hear from you and support you! To join, visit https://www.facebook.com/career_Rescue

In gratitude and with love,

Cassandra

P.S. If you're still teetering on the edge of change, don't worry. That's normal. Everything in good time. But take comfort if you're not yet in the right frame of mind.

It's hard to feel inspired, impossible to be creative, and challenging to feel confident, if you're trying to do everything on your own.

If you would like job search help, interview coaching or individual career advice please contact me by email (cassandra@cassandragaisford.com) or phone +64 21 873833. More information about my special coaching offer follows and at www.cassandragaisford.com.

ALSO BY THE AUTHOR

Mid-Life Career Rescue:

The Call for Change
What Makes You Happy
Employ Yourself
3 Book Box Set: The Call for Change, What Makes You Happy,
Employ Yourself

The Art of Living:

How to Find Your Passion and Purpose
Career Rescue: The Art and Science of Reinventing Your Career
and Life
Boost Your Self-Esteem and Confidence

The Art of Success:

Leonardo da Vinci

Coco Chanel

Journaling Prompts Series:

The Passion-Driven Business Planning Journal

Health & Happiness:

The Happy, Healthy Artist
Stress Less. Love Life More
Bounce: Overcoming Adversity, Building Resilience and Finding Joy

Mindful Sobriety:

Mind Over Mojitos: How Moderating Your Drinking Can Change Your Life:Easy Recipes for Happier Hours & a Joy-Filled Life
Your Beautiful Brain: Control Alcohol and Love Life More
Mind Your Drink: The Surprising Joy of Sobriety

Happy Sobriety:
Happy Sobriety: Non-Alcoholic Guilt-Free Drinks You'll Love
The Sobriety Journal
Happy Sobriety Two Book Bundle-Box Set: Alcohol and Guilt-Free Drinks You'll Love & The Sobriety Journal

Money Manifestation:
Financial Rescue: The Total Money Makeover: Create Wealth, Reduce Debt & Gain Freedom

The Prosperous Author:

Developing a Millionaire Mindset
Productivity Hacks: Do Less & Make More
The Prosperous Author-Two Book Bundle-Box Set (Books 1-2)

More of Cassandra's practical and inspiring workbooks on a range of career and life enhancing topics can be found on her website (www.cassandragaisford.com)   and   here —Author.to/CassandraGaisford

DEDICATION

*I dedicate this book to those of you
who are ready to live a beautiful life,
to stress less and do what others may say cannot be done.*

*This book is also for Lorenzo, my Knight Templar,
who encourages and supports me
to make my dreams possible...*

*And for all my clients
who have shared their dreams with me,
and allowed me to help them achieve amazing feats.*

Thank you for inspiring me.

PLEASE LEAVE A REVIEW

Your feedback encourages and sustains me and I love hearing from you.

Show your support. Share how this book has helped you by leaving a REVIEW—Even a one-liner would be helpful.

I recently received an email from a reader who said, *"Your books are a fantastic resource and until now I never even thought to write a review. Going forward I will be reviewing more books. So many great ones out there and I want to support the amazing people that write them."*

Great reviews also help people find good books.

THANK YOU

PS: If you enjoyed this book, do me a small favour to help spread the word about it and share news of this book with your tribe on Facebook, Twitter and other social networks.

FOLLOW YOUR PASSION TO PROSPERITY ONLINE COURSE

If you need more help to find and live your life purpose you may prefer to take my online course, and watch inspirational and practical videos and other strategies to help you to fulfill your potential.

Follow your passion and purpose to prosperity—online coaching program

Easily discover your passion and purpose, overcoming barriers to success, and create a job or business you love with my self-paced online course.

Gain unlimited lifetime access to this course, for as long as you like—across any and all devices you own. Be supported with practical, inspirational, easy-to-access strategies to achieve your dreams.

To start achieving outstanding personal and professional results with absolute certainty and excitement. **Click here to enroll or find out more— https://the-coaching-lab.teachable.com/p/follow-your-passion-and-purpose-to-prosperity**

ADDITIONAL HELP FROM CASSANDRA

EMPLOY YOURSELF! TRAIN TO BE A COACH

Is your job stressing you out? Cassandra is passionate about helping people change careers and create businesses they love and still pay the bills! If you share her passion and are seeking work that is fulfilling, financially rewarding and flexible becoming a career and life coach may be just what you have been looking for!
Work with passion and purpose!

Contact us to become an accredited:
- Career coach
- Life coach
- Happy at Work coach
- Creativity coach.

Navigate to: http://www.worklifesolutions.nz/coach-training

ONLINE CERTIFICATION COURSE NOW AVAILABLE

Discover how to make money as a life coach, earn extra income on the side, and easily create your own online business using the Work-life Solutions fail-proof system and attract your first paying client in weeks. All from the comfort of your own home or exotic destination.

Navigate to https://the-coaching-lab.teachable.com/p/worklife-solutions-coach-training-foundation-course

COACHING OFFER

I'm a woman on a mission.

I'm passionate about passion, joy and helping people stress less and live abundant, prosperous and beautiful love-filled lives. I know from experience this is possible for us all—and I also know from my personal and professional experience that it's hard to achieve on your own.

I love helping people discover their purpose, passion, and potential.

I love guiding people to find their beauty spot—that unique place that resides within us all, where talent, interest, and motivation inter-sect and enthusiasm collides.

I also adore coaching creative people and helping those with a passion for writing to bring their beautiful books into the world.

I've lived a chameleon life, shaping-shifting to find my place in life. I've had some horror jobs and experiences—and thankfully, some millionaire moments too. With over 25-years professional experience helping people transform their lives, as a holistic psychologist, career counselor, life coach, intuitive and bestselling author of self-empowerment and romance books. . .

. . .if you'd love to live a life of joy, fulfillment, and prosperity you're in good hands.

How we'll take your life to the next level

Often the thing getting in the way of finding your bliss is you! It's hard to step out of what you know or believe you are capable. Your mindset, beliefs and the old scripts that keep running through your head can hold you back. Unchallenged, your limited awareness can keep you, your dreams and your life small.

My strengths, expertise, and joys are awakening a sense of possibility, transforming your mindset, and helping you make the 'impossible' possible through solid, practical and proven strategies, branding and marketing so that you can build yourself a successful business and live the lifestyle you desire.

Whether you:

- Dream of creating a life you're passionate about
- Want to employ yourself or start a business on the side
- Yearn to be more creative
- Would love to write and successfully publish a book
- Fancy a career change and want to build a career you are proud of
- Would love to do what I do and become a transformational life and career coach
- Or just want to take your life to the next level, so you can build yourself a successful business and live the lifestyle you desire…

…you'll be inspired, feel empowered and succeed. Yes, it will take a commitment, but I promise you'll have fun and there will be passion and joy!

As Gary Keller writes in *The One Thing: The Surprisingly Simple Truth Behind Extraordinary Results*, a coach can spur you to better results. "Ideally, a coach can coach you on how to maximise your performance over time. This is how the very best become the very best," says Keller.

Commit to achieving extraordinary results and give your book the best chance possible.

"Thank YOU! Our coaching was immensely helpful, and I have renewed hope for finding my way. You are simply lovely, and brilliant, and wise. So glad our energies aligned, and I found you! I am also so enjoying your books and will give more feedback as I go as well as post reviews online. And they will be GLOWING, I can assure you!"
~ Lisa Webb, artist

"A coaching session with Cassandra is like a light switch to a light bulb. My ideas were there but without that light switch I wasn't able to see them and manifest my dream of running a holistic business from home. Straight away, Cassandra was able to get to the heart of my core values and how to put them into a dream business. I now have the sense of purpose and drive to achieve my business goals. Cassandra's warm personality and positive approach make her a joy to work with. I recommend her to anyone who wants to unlock their personal and professional potential."

~ Shelley Sweeney, writer & Reiki practitioner

Contact me at Cassandra@cassandragaisford.com to find out more. Or navigate to the following page to learn more about my coaching and how it can help you:

http://www.cassandragaisford.com/coaching/

(Did you know that coaching fees are often tax deductible for people who use coaching to improve their business and professional skills? Check with your accountant for details.)

ABOUT THE AUTHOR

Cassandra Gaisford, is a holistic psychologist, award-winning artist, and #1 bestselling author. A corporate escapee, she now lives and works from her idyllic lifestyle property overlooking the Bay of Islands in New Zealand.

Cassandra is best known for the passionate call to redefine what it means to be successful in today's world.

She is a well-known expert in the area of success, passion, purpose and transformational business, career and life change, and is regularly sought after as a keynote speaker, and by media seeking an expert opinion on career and personal development issues.

Cassandra has also contributed to international publications and been interviewed on national radio and television in New Zealand and America.

She has a proven-track record of success helping people find savvy ways to boost their finances, change careers, build a business or become a solopreneur—on a shoestring.

Cassandra's unique blend of business experience and qualifications (BCA, Dip Pych.), creative skills, and well-ness and holistic training (Dip Counselling, Reiki Master Teacher) blends pragmatism and commercial savvy with rare and unique insight and out-of-the-box-thinking for anyone wanting to achieve an extraordinary life.

Learn more about her on her website, her blog, or connect with her on Facebook and Twitter.

FURTHER RESOURCES MID-LIFE CAREER CHANGE

SURF THE NET

www.entrepreneur.com/howto—your go to place for all the latest tips and strategies from leading experts

www.gettingthingsdone.com—the official home of the work-life management system that has helped countless individuals and organizations bring order to chaos.

www.venusclubs.co.nz—a business community designed to help women in business thrive.

www.lifereimagined.org—loads of inspiration and practical tips to help you maximize your interests and expertize, personalized and interactive.

www.whatthebleep.com—a powerful and inspiring site emphasizing quantum physics and the transformational power of thought.

www.heartmath.org—comprehensive information and tools to help you access your intuitive insight and heart based knowledge. Validated and supported by science-based research.

www.personalitytype.com—owned by the authors of *Do What You Are: Discover the Perfect Career for You through the Secrets of*

Personality Type—this site focuses on expanding your awareness of your own type and that of others—including children and partners. This site also contains many useful links.

www.business.govt.nz/starting-and-stopping/entering-a-business/before-you-start-a-business—a New Zealand website with loads of tools and resources, including business plan templates, tips on how to choose a business name and more.

BOOKS—BUSINESS/PERSONAL SUCCESS

I read a book once. It changed my life. The ones below did too:

Retire Young, Retire Rich

Robert Kiyosaki; http://amzn.to/1P8r5bg

The 4-Hour Work Week: Escape the 9-5, Live Anywhere and Join the New Rich

Tim Ferris; *http://amzn.to/1P8nNok*

Think and Grow Rich

Napoleon Hill; *http://amzn.to/1nyW0Xc*

The Work We Were Born to Do

Nick Williams; http://amzn.to/1nyWQmL

The Business You Were Born to Create

Nick Williams; *http://amzn.to/1nyXkZU*

Trust Your Gut: How the Power of Intuition Can Grow Your Business

Lynn Robinson; http://amzn.to/1nyYJ2Q

Losing My Virginity: How I Survived, Had Fun, and Made A Fortune

Richard Branson: https://www.amazon.com/Losing-My-Virginity-Survived-Business/dp/0307720748

The 7 Habits of Highly Effective People

Stephen Covey; *http://amzn.to/1nyZjgO*

The Worrywart's Companion: Twenty-One Ways to Soothe Yourself and Worry Smart
Beverly A. Potter; http://amzn.to/1nyZVDc
Lovemarks: The Future Beyond Brands
Kevin Roberts, *http://amzn.to/1Kl3uaD*
Brain-Ding The Strategy: A Successful Marketing Plan Has to Include BRAIN-DING As The Ultimate Strategy
Francisco J. Serrano, http://amzn.to/1m7UMB6
Dream Big (Olivia)
Ian Falconer; http://amzn.to/1PsIS0D
It's Not How Good You Are, It's How Good You Want to Be
Paul Arden; http://amzn.to/1Kl4iwi
Steal Like an Artist
Austin Kleon; *http://amzn.to/1JWS90s*
Show Your Work
Austin Kleon; *http://amzn.to/1o4mm3N*
The Spontaneous Fulfilment of Desire: Harnessing the Infinite Power of Coincidence
Deeppak Chopra; *http://amzn.to/1meW1hW*
The Biology of Belief: Unleashing the Power of Consciousness, Matter & Miracles
Bruce Lipton; *http://amzn.to/1nQGXJ8*
StandOut 2.0: Assess Your Strengths, Find Your Edge, Win at Work
Marcus Buckingham; http://amzn.to/20PMrl9
Thrive:The Third Metric to Redefining Success and Creating a Happier Life
Arianna Huffington; http://amzn.to/1KJEmum

PLEASE LEAVE A REVIEW

Your feedback encourages and sustains me, and I love hearing from you.

Show your support. Share how this book has helped you by leaving a REVIEW—Even a one-liner would be helpful.

I recently received an email from a reader who said, *"Your books are a fantastic resource and until now I never even thought to write a review. Going forward I will be reviewing more books. So many great ones out there and I want to support the amazing people that write them."*

Great reviews also help people find good books.

Thank you

PS: If you enjoyed this book, do me a small favor to help spread the word about it and share links to purchase this book on Facebook, Twitter and other social networks.

STAY IN TOUCH

FOLLOW ME AND CONTINUE TO BE INSPIRED

www.cassandragaisford.com
www.twitter.com/cassandraNZ
www.instagram.com/cassandragaisford
www.facebook.com/cassandra.gaisford
http://www.youtube.com/cassandragaisfordnz
https://www.pinterest.com/cassandraNZ
www.linkedin.com/in/cassandragaisford

I invite you to share your stories and experiences in our Career Rescue Community. We'd love to hear from you! To join, visit https://www.facebook.com/career_Rescue

BLOG

Be inspired by regular posts to help you follow your bliss, slay self-doubt, and sustain healthy habits. You'll find a variety of articles and tips about people pursuing their passion and strategies to help you pursue yours—personally and professionally.

http://www.cassandragaisford.com

PRESENTATIONS

For information about products and workshops navigate to:
www.cassandragaisford.com/contact/speaking

To ask Cassandra to come and speak at your workplace or conference, contact: cassandra@cassandragaisford.com

ACKNOWLEDGMENTS

This book (and my new life) was made possible by the amazing generosity, open heartedness, and wonderful friendship of so many people. Thank you!

Sir Edmund Hillary often said that even Mount Everest wasn't climbed alone. A great achievement, or in my case a good book, is a product of collaboration. This project has, at times, loomed larger than the highest mountain in the world. I could not have persevered without the tremendous encouragement from a wealth of supportive and talented people.

To all the amazingly interesting clients who have allowed me to help them over the years, and to the wonderful people who read my newspaper columns and wrote to me with their stories of reinvention—thank you. Your feedback, deep sharing, requests for help, and inspired, courageous action continues to inspire me.

I'd also like to say a special thanks to the staff at *The Dominion Post* newspaper who gave me my first break into published writing. The *Mid-Life Carer Rescue* series would never have existed had they not acted on my suggestion that a careers column would be a great idea. For over four years they gave me the encouragement and artistic freedom to write freely on a range of topics—all with the goal of helping to encourage and inspire others.

I'm also grateful to the Health Editor of *Marie Claire* magazine whom, after she had accepted a short article, said I had the bones of a good book and should write it.

My thanks also to my terrific friends and supporters. And, of course, I can never say thank you enough to my family, particularly my parents and grandparents, who have instilled me with such tremendous values and life skills.

My daughter, Hannah—I wish for you everything that your heart desires. Without you, I doubt I would ever have accomplished all the things I have in my life.

Thank you.

Made in the USA
San Bernardino, CA
24 May 2019